Empath Overcoming Narcissist

A Recovery Guide to Reclaiming Your Power, Trusting Yourself Again, and Building a Beautiful Life After Narcissistic Abuse

Melissa DeVoe

Table of Contents

Introduction

Here's something that I want you to read. It's a journal entry from years back, just before I embarked on my healing journey. Years later, these words are still such a comfort to hear. They remain the softest place for me to land.

"Dear Melissa,

Today, I'm thinking and marveling at the courage and strength that you needed to get to this place. It requires a lot to leave a relationship with someone who can't or doesn't want to meet your needs. Facing that heartbreak is a brave thing to do right now so that in the future you don't have to struggle.

Sure, sometimes it feels selfish to put yourself first, but it will only seem that way until you realize how it changes your relationship with yourself and the people around you. Showing up for yourself empowers you to take the reins of your life and do a better job of showing up and loving the people in your life who truly matter."

Whenever I reflect on these words, they always take me back to a women empowerment workshop I attended. I started talking to this young lady who opened up to me about just having ended a 10-year relationship with a narcissistic and abusive partner. I saw so much of myself in her:

- the fixer who thought that she was capable of mending and fixing everybody else's brokenness

- the people pleaser who so desperately wants to be loved

- a girl who would bend and shape-shift herself for someone who would never love her in the way that she wanted to be loved

"What's one thing you wish someone would've taught or told you much sooner in life?" she asked me.

I, of course, didn't answer her right away. I wanted the depth of that question to sink in; to stew and marinate in that flow of emotion that I was feeling because I wanted what I was going to say next to be meaningful. And there was a lot that I wanted to say.

For starters, that you can't change the behavior of someone who isn't ready to change of their own volition. No amount of reasoning, argument, or justification will get them to see where you're coming from.

Secondly, that you don't have to apologize for setting boundaries with people, for wanting consistency in relationships, or for leaving relationships that are harmful to your mental health.

Instead, I settled and said this to her: "If there's one thing that I wished someone would have told me at an earlier age, it's this: that some relationships can't be mended. It's not our responsibility to fix people who don't want to take accountability for their own emotions."

Sometimes, we stay in toxic relationships knowing very well that they are not good for us—we allow our toxic partner to make us believe that the toxicity is all our fault. We allow them to tell us that we are too emotional, too uptight, or too needy. That is exactly what makes it hard for you to hold on to the version of reality that you're stuck with someone who isn't willing to take accountability for their part in the dynamic of your relationship.

The thing is, toxic people will often avoid taking accountability for their actions because they have an underlying need to control others and maintain power in their relationships. They engage in manipulative behaviors, such as gaslighting or blame-shifting, to avoid taking responsibility for their actions and make you feel responsible instead.

There are a few reasons why they do this:

1. **A need for control.** Toxic people often have a strong need for control in their relationships. They may view taking accountability as a sign of weakness and believe that it will diminish their power and control over their partner.

2. **Lack of empathy.** Toxic people often lack empathy for others and struggle to understand how their actions impact those around them. They may refuse to take accountability because they don't fully recognize the harm they have caused.

3. **Narcissism.** Some toxic people may have narcissistic tendencies and believe that they are always right. They may struggle to admit fault because it would require them to acknowledge that they are not perfect.

4. **Fear of abandonment.** Toxic people may fear losing their partner or being rejected if they admit fault. They may avoid taking accountability to protect themselves from the emotional pain of rejection.

Toxic people will avoid taking accountability because they prioritize their own needs and desires over the well-being of other people and the relationship. It's important to recognize these behaviors and take steps to protect yourself from emotional harm. This can include setting boundaries, seeking support from loved ones or a therapist, and potentially ending the relationship if the behavior continues.

If you're reading this right now and thinking to yourself that this is so you and you want to be free, then you're in luck. You need to allow yourself to heal from that relationship that was holding you prisoner. This is the exhale that you have been waiting for; the soft cushion to land on.

All that guilt that you are feeling for having allowed yourself to stay in a relationship that was unhealthy, I want you to put your hand on your chest and wait until you feel your heartbeat. As soon as you do, tell yourself that both the past and present versions of yourself deserve love and a whole lot of compassion too.

This is the time to reclaim our lives and I'm so glad and honored that you chose me to help you walk through this journey. I'm excited and so, so proud of you.

Chapter 1:

Your Gift Is Not a Curse

Some people are naturally more sensitive than others. Some of us get so quickly overwhelmed and bothered by things that would not necessarily bother others. Some of us feel things that other people don't necessarily feel or understand, and do you know what I want to tell you right now? I want to tell you that just because they don't understand doesn't mean that those feelings aren't valid. There is a place for your softness right here in this world.

As a highly sensitive person, I used to worry that the boundaries that I was setting with people were not valid. So, I would beat myself up for feeling too much all at once. *Why do you have to be like this?* I used to ask myself. But slowly, as I began to understand myself, the more I understood the people around me all that better as well. I learned that not all people are the same, and just because we don't all feel the same things, it doesn't mean you're less worthy.

To understand our softness, we have to understand what it means to be an empath. You might have been wondering if this is you but weren't initially all that sure. Let's take a look at what defines being an empath and the characteristics that are tied to it.

What It Means to Be an Empath

An empath is someone who has a high level of sensitivity to the emotions and energy of others, as well as the ability to intuitively understand and relate to those emotions. Empaths tend to feel the emotions of others deeply, often to the point where they can take on the emotions themselves (Raypole, 2019). Some common characteristics of empaths are discussed below.

Highly Intuitive

Empaths have a strong intuition and can quickly pick up on the emotions and energies of others. Being highly intuitive means having a strong sense of inner knowing and relying on your intuition to guide your thoughts, feelings, and actions. Intuition is a natural ability that allows us to understand and perceive things without conscious reasoning or analysis. It is often described as "gut feeling" or "inner voice" and can provide valuable insights and guidance in various aspects of life, including relationships, career choices, personal growth, and decision-making.

Highly intuitive individuals usually pick up on subtle cues from their environment or interpersonal interactions, allowing them to read people's emotions, motives, and intentions. They may also have a deep sense of empathy and connect with others on an emotional level. Intuitive people often trust their instincts and are comfortable making decisions based on their inner guidance, even if it goes against logical reasoning or conventional wisdom.

Being highly intuitive can be a valuable asset in many areas of life, as it allows us to tap into our inner wisdom, connect more deeply with others, and make decisions that are aligned with our true selves.

Sensitive

Empaths are highly sensitive to the emotions, energies, and environments around them. Essentially, when you are a highly sensitive person, your body and your mind respond more differently to the world around you. You feel heartbreak, pain, and loss at a much more intense level than anyone else. You become more responsive to the world around you.

Being a sensitive person may also mean that you need to spend more time alone than most people do. You are more affected by other people's moods than most people. You easily become overstimulated.

I realize that honoring my sensitivity has played such a significant role in my breaking up from my people-pleasing patterns. I spent so many years trying to deny myself my sensitivities to make other people feel more comfortable. My world changed dramatically when I realized that I don't have to do that anymore. In some way or another, relationships do require some measure of sacrifice. But what a lot of us sensitive people do is overdo it.

We have to remember that we are allowed to compromise in our relationships. We just need to make sure that we don't do it to the point where we are unrecognizable. What we can do instead is honor our sensitivities by setting boundaries. You can do this by:

- not squeezing more plans into a schedule that is already full

- taking time alone when you need it most; even if it means that other people will need to find a way to occupy their time without you

- reducing the time that you spend around people and environments that are emotionally draining for you

- honoring the sanctity of your workspaces and work environments and being more intentional about who you choose to let in your life

I want you to remember that your sensitivity is a big part of who you are. And you should never in any way or form ever be ashamed of that. Family, culture, and your origin stories may have "encouraged" you to pick up a shame-based approach to your sensitivity, but there is no such thing as being "too sensitive." You are entitled to your place of feeling. No one gets to be a gatekeeper of your emotions.

These are labels defined and created by people who are out of tune with their own emotions. These are people with a limited capacity to feel or regulate their own emotions; people who have learned that it is not safe to show any vulnerability—ever. There is nothing wrong with you. You are sensitive and that is a beautiful thing, so continue setting and enforcing the boundaries that you must.

It's quite hard and awkward in those initial stages. You'll guilt-trip yourself, but over time, the people who are closest to you'll begin to understand and understand that you're doing all of these things out of love; for yourself and them as well. It's all about designing a lifestyle that leaves enough room for your sensitivities, instead of one that forces you to shrink them.

Emotional Depth

Empaths tend to feel emotions deeply and have strong emotional reactions to situations. Empaths are special in the sense that they carry within them an intense ability to interpret and carry emotions in ways that other people don't necessarily know how to. This matters because being in tune with our emotions leads to the following:

- **Allows us to connect to the people in our lives who matter more.** Relationships, be they platonic or romantic, thrive when we can empathize with one another. People want to feel heard. They want to be seen and understood and when you find the kind of people who are willing to make and leave that much space open for us, we thrive.

- **Greater self-awareness.** This is one of my favorite expressions—something that I tell myself every single day before I go to bed and just before I get up: "I'm connected to me; therefore, I won't lose myself because this heart, this mind, and this intuition know where they are leading me to."

  Emotional depth allows us to connect to the deepest parts of who we are; it allows us to understand our feelings and motivations and provides much insight into the reasons why we do the things we do. We can't heal what we don't understand. So, knowing what it is that I need to look into allows us to implement and put into action the steps that will help us become better versions of who we are meant to be.

- **Enhanced creativity.** As an empath, I find so much comfort in being able to express and live out my experiences through words. Words are healing and they also provide that kind of comfort that reminds us that we are not alone. Emotional depth can stimulate creativity and allows us to tap into that well of authenticity that resides within us; be it through art, music, writing, and even dance. It allows us to be who we are meant to be.

- **Better decision-making.** Our emotions are emotions and that's that. They don't get to define our worth and don't say anything about our characters Sometimes, when we are upset or experiencing a particularly difficult emotion, we tend to be impulsive and do things that we end up regretting later. Being in tune with our emotions allows us to think first before we act or speak because that kind of closeness with our emotions allows us to understand that our choices don't just impact us but others as well.

- **Improved mental health.** We become stronger and better people when we realize that we will still see hard days, but that doesn't have to be what defines us. Accepting that life is a roller-coaster ride will equip us with the strength that we need to handle those bad days more productively when they happen to us. This naturally leads to improved self-esteem and a greater sense of purpose and meaning in life.

That strong connection that I have with my emotions has taught me that the thing that I don't have to apologize for is wanting consistency in my relationships.

I don't have to be upset about being reactive to toxic people or situations.

I don't have to apologize for leaving relationships that are harmful to my mental health—or having opinions that differ from other people's. I have certainly come a long way. I'm stronger and quite frankly, I'm a lot braver than I was a couple of years back. When I look back to those past versions of myself, my heart tends to break just a little. But I'm glad that I'm no longer at that place. By choosing to not apologize for those parts of us that deserve to exist, we are acknowledging that our presence has a purpose.

Fiercely Compassionate

Empaths are compassionate and care deeply about others. They can intuitively understand others' needs and emotions. Kindness is something that will never go out of style. Sometimes, I think to myself that besides the essentials that we need to survive, the only other thing that matters is the compassion that we carry for one another.

This is because people out here are going through some tough times; they are carrying backbreaking baggage they couldn't possibly carry alone. So, compassion matters because it helps us to foster generosity toward others and to help them when they are in need.

Recharging

Empaths often need time alone to recharge their emotional batteries, as they can become overwhelmed by the emotions of others. I'm very much an "I'll text you" or a "I'll call you back later" kind of person.

Love for Nature

Many empaths find peace and comfort in nature as it provides a sense of calm and natural energy.

Being an empath can be both a blessing and a curse because the ability to understand and relate to others on an intimate level comes with its own set of emotional struggles. But with the right tools and support, we can learn to harness our unique abilities and thrive in our personal and professional lives.

Challenges of Being an Empath

Being an empath, like everything else, comes with its own set of obstacles. While we've mentioned some of them so far, below we'll break down common daily challenges you'll likely face.

Distinguishing Between Emotions

We have difficulties distinguishing between our emotions and those of others due to our high sensitivity. Whenever I'm talking to someone, the natural thing for me to want to do is to relate to that person's emotions on a personal level. It's my way of validating their experiences. It's my way of letting them know that I see them—that I understand them and am there for them.

Because of that, I end up personalizing those emotions and carrying them. But, I've come to learn that it is possible to be there and to support people without taking over their loads. I'm not responsible for fixing or for finding solutions to other people's problems or pains. Rather, I can offer as much support as I can without allowing it to affect me negatively.

It's easier for us to be overwhelmed by negative emotions. We tend to absorb sadness, anxiety, and anger if we're being honest with one another. They're quite draining and exhausting to carry—especially when they aren't our own. When we start to feel the negative weight of those emotions pressing in on us, we must learn to step back.

We won't ever be able to show up for people the way that they want us to show up for them if we aren't taking care of ourselves properly. This overwhelm of emotion might cause or lead us to become resentful people in the future. This is not a realistic expectation that we should have of ourselves or anyone else for that matter.

If you're in a position or place where someone wants more than you can give, here are a couple of helpful statements that you can go to: "I feel for you and can't imagine how hard this must be for you, but right now, I'm not in an emotionally healthy place. So, there isn't much that I can offer other than the fact that I'm here and thinking of you."

Difficulty in Setting Boundaries

Guilt, more often than not, is the obstacle that is holding us back from setting the boundaries that we need. As empaths, we have a strong desire to help others, we want to show up and shine for our people because we know how incredibly lonely it is to not have people in your corner. This often leads to us overextending ourselves and neglecting our own needs. We put people first even when it doesn't benefit our well-being.

Another reason why we rarely enforce and set boundaries like we need to is that we have a crippling fear of rejection or conflict. It prevents us from asserting ourselves and setting clear boundaries in the situations that we need to. And finally, this is one that I can strongly relate to and resonate with. We feel guilty or selfish for prioritizing our own needs over others', leading to a sense of internal conflict and confusion.

Here's the thing, when our needs go unmet—in a platonic or romantic relationship—attempting to find a solution that isn't messy or complicated can leave us in a bad space for years. Sometimes, we have to choose between these two pains: the pain of staying in that place that has robbed you of your privilege to breathe, or the pain of leaving and starting someplace anew again.

I often say to people that sometimes boundaries work and other times they don't because we can't force people to change if they're stuck in their ways. They have to want to change for the boundaries to truly work. That is when we have to acknowledge that "This is my cue to go." The choice won't always be, "How do I avoid the pain of [situation X or Y]?" but rather, "If I were loving myself well right now, which pain would I rather choose?"

Feeling Isolated or Misunderstood

It's easy to feel isolated or misunderstood because our sensitivity to the emotions of others may not always be understood or valued by others. How many times have you shared something with a partner and had them say something along the lines of, "But don't you just think that you're overreacting about this" or "Don't you think that you're making a big deal out of nothing?"

Honestly, it's such a huge red flag when you share something with someone—be it an accomplishment or good news and you end up getting a half-assed fake reaction. As empaths, it can be quite difficult for us to understand why someone else would be devastated at the thought of our success—that's simply because of our wiring. What narcissistic people do is take that information and go on to later use it against us. They will manipulate and twist our words.

This is something that can erode our sense of safety and trust—leaving long-lasting wounds. Mocking someone's reaction, regardless of how insignificant it may seem, is never an okay thing to do. We can't make other people honor our feelings. We can't make them take any accountability, but we can choose to empower ourselves by deciding how close and connected we're willing to stay next to that person who invalidates our feelings in our toughest moments.

For some people, most situations are either black or white; it's this or that and nothing else in between, but for an empath, it's not always the case and that is why we sometimes have difficulty in making decisions: We can see multiple perspectives and that makes us feel the emotions associated with each option.

We are also deeply afraid of hurting other people. That's why we always put them first., It's because we believe that we need a special reason to prioritize our own needs, but we don't. It's okay to not show up for people when you can't. It's okay to disappoint some people. It's okay to simply say, "I can't do this," or, "I don't want to do this." Is it going to be easy at first? No. But we have to first and foremost continually remind ourselves that we belong to ourselves... And no one else.

Next time, when you're not willing to do something, speak up by saying, "I don't have the mental capacity for this right now. It won't work for me." Don't offer false promises and agree to something that will make you resent yourself later.

Dearest empath, honoring yourself means that you are going to be the big bad villain in someone else's story. The truth is, not everyone will like us. Sometimes, honoring ourselves is going to mean disappointing someone, canceling plans, or telling someone that you can't help them out with something. We are allowed to hold our version of reality. There is nothing that hurts more than that pain of self-betrayal.

The Narcissist

Let's talk about the narcissist: the person who will always find fault in something. The people who will always criticize you, put you down, and bring out your most painful wounds then throw them in your face. Narcissists are always playing out their most toxic projections. Their unhealed parts are eating them alive.

Their outer ego is essentially screaming all the time, "You have to comply with this. You are the one who has to take my pain away. You must obey. You must be subservient. You must go above and beyond what I say you need to confirm my significance."

They constantly do put-downs and display awful behavior. They project their most damaged parts. When you find yourself in this battle, it won't always be easy to see the truth of it. When you spend the majority of your time in the presence of a blood-sucking vampire, you are naturally going to start believing things that you never thought you'd believe and start behaving in ways that you thought you would never behave.

You'll find yourself at a point and place thinking, *Oh my word, is this something that I really did?* That's why you need to know how to figure out how to pick one out of a crowd. You'll thank me later.

To spot a narcissist, you need to look out for these key signs:

- They will at any given chance always choose to play the victim.

- They will always act like they have empathy, but in reality, they have none or any conscience whatsoever.

- They have a humble demeanor. Essentially, they may come across as vulnerable, open, and sensitive, but upon clever observation, their intense resentment and jealousy will start to show.

- They do things for others, but they expect something in return.

- Image is more important than anything and they like to have that reputation for being a nice person.

- They are passive-aggressive and don't deal with conflict in a way that they really should.

In healthy relationships we:

- Make space for each other's goals and dreams.

- We respect and value our partners for who they are. We offer an environment that is enriching for all of us to be in. We engage in mutual giving and taking and don't just expect one person in the relationship to do everything.

- We make space for each of our complex emotions and respect the boundaries that we enforce and set for one another.

- We show up as our most authentic selves and make a habit out of communicating our needs, values, and boundaries. With narcissists, there is none of that. It's all about them; there is no resolution or working together. They'll never apologize, introspect, or change their behavior, even when they know that they need to change their behaviors.

Fatal Attraction

The thing about narcissists is that they are incredibly good at sussing out our deepest vulnerabilities. It's almost like a sixth sense of theirs. They prey on that tenderness—on our gentle nature and vulnerabilities.

They do that as a means of gaining power and control in relationships. Vulnerabilities can include emotional, psychological, or physical weaknesses, such as low self-esteem, anxiety, depression, or past trauma.

Narcissists are often skilled at identifying and exploiting these vulnerabilities in others and may use tactics such as gaslighting, manipulation, and emotional abuse to control their victims. They may also use flattery, charm, and other forms of love bombing to initially win over their targets.

It's important to note that anyone can be vulnerable at different times in their lives, and having vulnerabilities doesn't make a person weak or deserving of mistreatment. However, being aware of one's vulnerabilities can help individuals to recognize and avoid potentially toxic relationships, and to seek support and resources to address any underlying issues.

If you suspect that you or someone you know is in a relationship with a narcissist, it's important to seek help from a trusted friend, family member, or professional. Narcissistic abuse can be very damaging to a person's mental and emotional well-being, and it's important to take steps to protect oneself and seek healing.

Here is a summary of reasons why narcissists are often drawn to empaths:

- Narcissists are often drawn to empaths because empaths tend to be compassionate, caring, and understanding individuals who are highly attuned to the emotions of others. This can be very appealing to narcissists, who are often looking for people who can provide them with a constant source of attention, admiration, and validation.

- Empaths also tend to be very giving and may be willing to put the needs of others before their own. This can make them vulnerable to the manipulations of narcissists, who may take advantage of their kindness and generosity.

- In addition, empaths may be more likely to forgive and overlook the negative behaviors of others, which can provide narcissists with a sense of power and control in the relationship. Narcissists may also be drawn to the empath's ability to provide emotional support and validation, as they often crave attention and approval.

It's important to note that not all empaths are necessarily susceptible to the manipulations of narcissists and that healthy relationships are built on mutual respect and trust. It's also important for empaths to set healthy boundaries and to be aware of their own needs and feelings in any relationship.

The one thing that you don't even have to feel guilty about is removing toxic people from your life, regardless of their relationship with you. It could've been a family member, partner, or friend that you've known since childhood. You don't owe space to anyone who causes you pain or belittles your existence.

It's great if they decide to take accountability for their behavior and strive for change, but if they blatantly disrespect your emotions, ignore the boundaries that you set, and persist in harming you, darling, it's time to let them go.

Chapter 2:

To Hell and Back

Your feelings are valid. You shouldn't have to feel guilty about the way you feel. The one thing some of my friends used to tell me when I was still working through my healing journey was this: "Well, at least he wasn't hitting you and I get it." They thought that they were saying the statements from a place of love and consideration, but the one thing that they failed to understand is that abuse isn't only about whether or not they were hitting you.

It's not just about surviving the trauma or the aftermath. It's about surviving the instances where your nervous system is constantly bracing you for it to happen again. It's about not being able to rest or constantly filled with panic. It's about feeling as if you're deprived of oxygen 24/7.

I'm a survivor. It took me years to get to the place where I am right now. I stayed in a toxic relationship that left me feeling for years that that kind of behavior was normal or that I deserved it. So, before we delve further into this topic, I want you to remember a few special and empowering reminders if you have ever found yourself in a position and situation like mine. Whether you are struggling to find your way out or learning to find your footing, these words will give you the reassurance that you need.

I'm a strong woman. This is the thought that has to be at the forefront of your morning when you wake up—when you make your morning cuppa. Why? When you build and champion yourself, it's going to encourage you to keep going. You'll be less likely to be tempted to give up on yourself, but rather, motivated to keep going and to seek the healing that you need.

I deserve the kind of love that treats me with tenderness. With compassion. With care and consideration. The thing about abusive partners or relationships is that they will leave us feeling like we are deserving of the bare minimum. That we are undeserving of the good things that are trying to find their way to us, but that isn't true.

You are a whole and remarkable human and anyone who knows you understands what a rare gem you are. So, don't diminish your worth because of what you went through. Don't be convinced that you deserve to be in the backseat at all times. There's someone out there who admires you and is in awe of your remarkable strength.

Your past doesn't define you. I hope that you find enough space for yourself to thrive and live life despite all that has happened to you. I hope you offer yourself grace in an overflow. I hope you allow all of the hardened places within you to soften. Be kinder to yourself. You and only you are the one who should and gets to define your worth. Period. So, fight. Fight for yourself and don't give up.

You are loved and wholeheartedly so. There are people out there who would walk to the ends of the earth just to see you smile. Friends, family, acquaintances, and coworkers are all alike. So, don't you for a second entertain the thought that you don't matter. Not one single time. Your existence has a place here on this earth. You are so welcome here. You are incredible, and one day, I hope that you have the courage and strength to look in the mirror and tell yourself, "You are loved."

It's okay if you're still learning to figure things out or find who you are. I mean, that abuser took so much of your identity away from you, so it's okay to take time and go through that journey of exploration all again. Also, know that it is normal to decide at any point in time that you want to change your mind about something. It's okay if you want to take your time to think through certain things.

Laughter is a part of healing too. Would you believe me if I told you that for the longest time throughout my healing journey, I used to tell myself that I was simply just not allowed to be happy? I felt that laughter or moments of rejoicing were essentially invalidating the experience I went through. But what I realized was that by denying myself that opportunity to laugh and rejoice, I would be doing myself the greatest injustice.

You don't need to be working on getting better every single day, 24/7. That was my biggest mistake. I thought that healing was something that I needed to be working on every single day of my life, but it doesn't have to be that way. Some days are undoubtedly going to be faster or slower than others. But, throughout the journey, remember that it's okay to come up for air—to breathe and rest because that too is also what healing is all about.

Don't you ever doubt your place in this world. You are needed. You are so very much appreciated and mean so much to the people around you.

Life does and will get better. It won't always be this hard, even though it currently feels that way to you. These hard days and tough times are just here to remind us of our resilient and remarkable spirits.

You can't unlearn a series of negative coping mechanisms in a matter of days. It's going to take months and, sometimes, even years. That unlearning and becoming is complex, complicated, and very messy, so be patient and kind to yourself along your journey.

As long as your efforts are consistent and you are choosing to dwell on new thoughts, feelings, and actions, you will get there.

If you're still hurting right now, I want you to remember that things won't always be this way and that those things won't always hurt this much. We change and we grow. We live and we learn. In life, we often experience things or situations that we feel are literally going to be the end of it. We go about our days thinking to ourselves, *I can't possibly imagine myself being okay from all of this*. But you know what, a couple of months, or even weeks down the line, you get to a point and you can't help but think to yourself, *Oh my gosh. I made it*.

You start laughing and smiling a whole lot more. You realize that you are happier and more at peace and that you feel alive in the most remarkable way. You realize that yes, those bad times are a part of your story, but they are certainly not what gets to define you. You realize that the little voice that was always whispering in your ear was right all along. You really are that brave.

Why It's Not So Easy to Leave

One of the other most common questions that people ask abuse survivors is: "But why didn't you leave any sooner if things were that bad?" And I'll tell you this one thing. It's not easy to leave an abusive relationship as it's a messy process that takes time because of fear. I used to be deathly afraid of what he would do if I tried to leave. Would things become a lot more physical? Would he retaliate?

These are just some of the thoughts that go through your mind when you think about leaving. Below, we'll discuss isolation, financial dependence, and trauma bonding as some of the reasons for not leaving.

Isolation

Abusers understand that you are at your weakest when you are alone. That is why they will do things to isolate you from your friends and family. This makes it harder for you to seek out the support that you truly need.

Financial Dependence

Some abusers want you to be entirely dependent on them— emotionally and financially. They want to leave you with as few resources as possible so that you continually return to them.

Trauma Bonding

What is trauma bonding? This is a term used to describe a situation where a strong emotional attachment forms between two people, often in a toxic relationship. This bond is typically characterized by a cycle of abuse and affection, where the abuser alternates between demonstrating love and kindness and inflicting emotional, physical, or sexual harm.

Over time, you become dependent on them for validation and emotional support, which leads to a deep and complex bond that can be difficult to break. You start to rationalize their behavior or even blame yourself for the abuse, further reinforcing the bond.

Trauma bonding can happen in any relationship, including romantic partnerships, parent-child relationships, and even in cases of kidnapping or hostage-taking. It's a significant barrier to leaving an abusive relationship because you feel trapped by your emotional attachment to the abuser.

Also helpful to know are the signs that you might actually be in a trauma bond with the abuser. Here are some signs:

- You don't like the person but you still choose to stay with them.

- They are only "sometimes abusive" and that's why you choose to stay with them because it's not such a regular occurrence.

- Disturbing things happen to you, but you still choose to brush them off as "nothing."

- Your friends and family encourage you to leave, but you choose to stay with the person.

The one thing that I have come to learn is that oftentimes, our tendency to lose ourselves in other people has got very little to do with our relationship with that person. But more so, it is often about the fact that we have become accustomed to the toxic environment that they have created.

The shame, guilt, and critical self-talk drive us further away from us, prompting us to further seek refuge and shelter in the home of the "abuser." Because when we haven't yet learned how to create a safe home for ourselves, we will go around seeking shelter in other places, even if those places are toxic.

As an abuse survivor who once found herself caught in the web of a trauma bond, my hope and goal are to bring more awareness to this vicious cycle of abuse that keeps us shackled. So, here are the stages of trauma bonding (Laub, 2022):

1. **Love bombing.** They will shower you with love and promise you the ends of the earth. This love and affection make you feel special and appreciated. This is the equivalent of the honeymoon phase. It's a manipulation tactic that is set to simply just win you over.

2. **Dependency and trust.** One thing about abusers is that they will go out of their way to get you to trust them. They're going to make you dependent on their lives and their validation. You might also hear them often say things like "I'll never stop loving you." It's like things go from 0–100 so quickly and you also start to believe that no one will love you the way they do.

3. **Devaluation stage.** A chameleon doesn't hide its colors for too long. Sooner or later, the criticism will come. They start chipping away at your confidence by critiquing the way you speak, how you act, or the friends you spend your time with. They blame you for small things that aren't even your fault. This is where you start to believe that there is truth in what they are saying and you too start to blame yourself.

4. **Gaslighting.** This is where they start denying you the validity of your own experiences. They tell you that you are just being dramatic, that you are overreacting and making a big deal out of nothing. But in reality, what is happening is that they are gradually separating you from your friends and your family. You then feel more alone than ever because they prey on that loneliness that comes from being isolated.

   Here are six common types of gaslighting that can show up in a relationship (Glass, 2022):

a. **Countering.** This can show up in things such as them questioning your memory, which then obviously leads to you questioning your reality. Here is an example of what that might sound like in an actual conversation: "But I can't put any trust in what you're saying right now. You never seem to remember anything. There's always something that you're forgetting."

b. **Withholding.** They will refuse to engage in any conversation with you. Or they deflect from situations or altogether avoid talking about certain topics. Let's say you want to broach the subject of how they're always losing their temper or how it seems like they are always trying to blame you for things that aren't even your fault. You might hear them say something like: "Well, I have absolutely no idea what you're talking about. You aren't making any sense."

c. **Trivializing.** This has to be one of the most common forms of gaslighting. A toxic partner will always try to invalidate and make it seem as though your feelings aren't valid. They will always make you feel as if you're making an unnecessarily big deal out of things that shouldn't even be that big of a deal. "You're being too sensitive," "Calm down," or "It's not even that big of a deal." Does that sound familiar?

d. **Denial.** Accountability, quite frankly, is something that is not in a narcissist's vocabulary. They will at all and any costs deny that they said something, and, as usual, claim that you are making things up. "You're being delusional right now. I would never say something like that."

e. **Diversion.** Changing the topic is their way of making you question your credibility. The thing with the narcissist is that they are also obsessed with control. It makes them feel threatened when they aren't in full control of the conversation. Diversion is also their way of avoiding any responsibility for their actions as well as trying to manipulate you into thinking a certain way. A frequent statement that might show up here is "Oh, there you go making something up again."

f. **Stereotyping.** They will at any cost use negative stereotypes to manipulate you. This includes anything like your age, gender, sexuality, or ethnicity. For example, "You're way too young to understand what I'm talking about here. or oh, I forgot, you're a woman. I wouldn't expect you to understand."

5. **Resigning control.** At this stage, you eventually give up believing in yourself and the perception that belongs fully to you. You start to feel a lack of trust in yourself. It becomes a lot easier for you to give in to that person's requests. You find that it becomes a lot harder for you to even make your own decisions. This is where the concept of self-gaslighting also comes in. Here are some examples of how you may start to gaslight yourself in the relationship:

- You start blaming or criticizing yourself for not handling things a lot differently.

- You start to criticize yourself for being overly sensitive or too dramatic without actually checking in on your feelings, figuring out where they come from, or seeing if there is any validity to them.

- You start shaming yourself for being too needy; for being too much without acknowledging or embracing the fact that you are a human being with unmet needs and it is those very unmet needs that are driving this behavior that you are shaming yourself for.

- You blame or shame yourself for not leaving the person soon enough, even though you can feel that they are in no way healthy for you. You fail to realize or acknowledge that their toxic behavior has a profound impact on you—it's not just something that you get over so quickly.

6. **Losing yourself.** They have broken down and chipped away at any ounce of self-confidence that you have. You have surrendered and given up on standing up for yourself because all that it does is makes matters worse. You feel withdrawn and lost. You're constantly apologizing even for things that need no apologizing.

7. **Emotional addiction.** Abusive relationships feel like an emotional roller-coaster ride. You start to develop an emotional dependency on that person. The abuser in some way becomes your reason for "being." Depression and anxiety start to take their toll on you. You feel broken and it feels like the only person who is capable of "fixing" you is them.

Breaking a Trauma Bond

The fear of the unknown is more often than not what keeps us stuck in these toxic and limiting relationships. It's what makes us rationalize irrational things and settle for the toxicity in that relationship. But we must remind ourselves that the closing of one door often means that another one gets to open. So, walking away from a toxic situation or relationship essentially means that you'll be walking toward a healthier and much happier you; you're walking toward connections that you wholeheartedly deserve.

Breaking a trauma bond with a narcissist is possible. I remember thinking that there was something wrong with me because why would anyone in their right mind want to go back to someone who was causing them so much grief and pain? But, I continue to reassure that part of me that needed kindness the most that healing was possible. I reassured that part of me that we would recover.

See the person for who they truly are and not for what you want them to be. There is nothing like a person who is sometimes empathetic and sometimes abusive. There is no in-between. Period. It might be difficult to integrate this retaliation into everyday life, but it will be helpful further along your healing journey.

Learn to understand that the part of you that returns to them—the part that feels that it can't live without that person—is not a healthy part of you. It is a part of your psyche that needs nurturing and loving-kindness; it's a part that needs reparenting from the part of your brain that is more emotionally mature to help soothe and change those behaviors.

It's important to remember that leaving an abusive relationship is a process, and it often takes time and support from others to do so safely.

Understanding the Types of Abuse That a Narcissist Inflicts

When we hear the word "abuse," our minds naturally go to the physical and sexual kind. However, we must understand that abuse manifests in a number of forms, such as psychological, emotional, and financial, to name a few. Below is a brief overview of each type of abuse.

Emotional Abuse

Healing from emotional abuse has taught me a lot of things; more so the things that I do not have to apologize for. Those things are:

- My feelings.

- Having firm boundaries.

- Saying no to things that I'm not interested in doing.

- Small things like not answering the phone when I don't feel like it.

- Saying my word when I know that things don't feel right. I don't have to blame myself for how other people behave or act. I don't have to feel guilty for putting myself first.

- For not settling for less than I deserve.

- For letting go when I need to and moving through life at a pace that feels right and easy to me.

Signs of Emotional Abuse

Emotional abuse is the equivalent of a thousand cuts. It eats away at us until we get to a point or start to feel like we can't possibly go at this life thing all on our own. The most common signs of emotional abuse are:

- **Your partner yelling at you.** It's normal now and again for you and your partner to raise voices in the relationship, but what isn't normal or healthy in any way is turning every disagreement into a shouting match. Yelling is an unproductive way to deal with disagreements in relationships and it also creates an imbalance of power where the person who yells the loudest is the one who gets heard.

- **Contempt.** It's not easy to feel happy for your partner if you feel a sense of contempt whenever you see that person. It also becomes difficult for the other person to express their feelings and to have the other person listen. In healthy relationships, there should be an equal amount of give and take; and listening and talking. So, when there is sarcasm or arrogance from one party, it creates a barrier to healthy communication.

- **Threats.** Narcissists will often use threats to get you to do what they want: "If you don't do [this], I'm going to do [that]…" In doing so, they back you into a corner and leave you feeling like you have no other option (Gordon, 2019).

Financial Abuse

A narcissistic partner loves to use money as a weapon because they know just how essential it is. They want to have power over another person because they want to feel better about themselves. One of the easiest ways to do this is by controlling finances. Financial abuse from a narcissistic partner will often look like a lot of things, but generally, it will involve the controlling or manipulating of finances in a way that puts you on the negative side of things (Hammond, 2015).

Some common examples of financial abuse by a narcissistic partner include:

- **Controlling access to money**

The narcissist will want to control all aspects of the finances and limit their partner's access to money. They may also withhold money as a form of punishment or use the money to manipulate their partner's behavior. Another thing about having a narcissistic partner is that they can be overly and incredibly generous when it comes to money when they are in public. For example, they will be quick to cover the costs of a dinner for a colleague or they might only just give gifts for show.

This experience and behavior from their side can be incredibly isolating because it warps your reality on how things are really like. Just imagine how confusing and frustrating it must feel to have a partner who insists on paying for dinner for friends, but then, on the way back home you have to listen to them rant about all of the people who are freeloading from you guys.

- **Sabotaging your employment**

You having your own job or career means that you will be independent and that when you do decide to leave them, you will have something to fall back on. That is something that they don't want. They want you to be entirely dependent on them. So, they may sabotage your employment opportunities, making it difficult for them to earn money or advance their career.

They'll say things like: "But I don't think that's an appropriate job title for you. Why would you want to apply for a job when you have me to support you?" They'll even go so far as to tell you that you aren't talented enough and that by applying for that promotion, all that you're doing is setting yourself up for failure and disappointment.

- **Running up debt in your name**

We've already established that a narcissist is selfish and self-absorbed. They do things that negatively impact you, but they don't want to experience any of the side effects. They may run up debt in your name (open up credit cards or take loans in your name, or even go so far as to use your credit cards without permission, leaving you with the financial burden of their spending.

The narcissist is hypocritical in the sense that they believe that the rules do not and should not apply to them in any form or way. So, when it comes to budgeting, they will be too quick to enforce rules and to tell you what you can and can't do, but when it comes to them, they will go ahead and spend freely without worrying or thinking about the consequences in any way.

They will go out to eat at all the fancy places and buy themselves all kinds of luxury items, but they'll go ahead and criticize you for making the smallest of purchases.

- **Using financial dependence as a weapon**

They may force you to depend on them financially, threatening to withhold money or support you if you don't comply with their demands. They will reward and punish you with anything that is money-related. For example, they will plan something nice for you and once you guys have argued, they will then go on and tell you that you are the one who has to pay for the expenses.

- **Financial infidelity**

When you are in a relationship with someone, both of you have to learn to be open about your finances, especially if the relationship that you're in is something that you would like to go on for the long haul, but what a narcissistic partner does is hide their financial activities from you, including having secret bank accounts, investments or other financial assets.

Keeping you in the dark enables them to make one-sided decisions. This then controls your perception of what you guys can and can't afford. "I'll worry about the finances so that you don't have to stress that much about them" or "You're better with things that need managing around the house. Let me take care of all the money issues."

Remember, it's okay to let your partner help you manage finances if you don't feel that comfortable managing them yourself. But that often has negative consequences. For example, if they end up not paying the bills on time, it can end up causing some serious damage to your credit score. Always try to be involved if any financial decisions, in particular, affect you.

Physical Abuse

If you have to change your behavior because you are scared of how your partner is going to act or what they are going to do to you if you don't do something in the way that they want you to, then that is a sign that you are being abused.

Narcissists use physical abuse as a means of control and domination over you. They may use physical violence to intimidate, punish, or coerce their partners or family members into doing what they want. Narcissists may also use physical abuse as a way to demonstrate their power and superiority over others (Hammond, 2015).

Physical abuse can take many forms, including hitting, slapping, punching, kicking, choking, and using weapons. Narcissists may also engage in less obvious forms of physical abuse, such as withholding food or medical care or forcing their victims to engage in sexual acts against their will.

It's important to note that not all narcissists use physical violence, and not all people who use physical violence are narcissists.

Sexual Abuse

Most people, especially women who are in romantic relationships, do not realize that just because you are married to someone, just because someone has been your partner for X number of years, they do not own your body. Your body is your body and anyone who wants to be with you or wants to touch you has to get your consent, first and foremost.

Narcissists may use sexual abuse as a means of exerting power and control over their victims. Sexual abuse can take many forms, including but not limited to sexual assault, rape, sexual harassment, and sexual coercion.

Sexual abuse is a narcissist's tactic to manipulate and exploit you. They want you to feel powerless and vulnerable. They use their charm and charisma to gain your trust and then they later use that to coerce or force you into sexual acts they do not want to engage in. Sometimes, the sexual abuse might show up in them saying things like: "Oh, but to show that you love me, you'll [do this] in bed for me" or "You're my wife [or girlfriend], you have to sleep with me."

Narcissists also use sexual abuse as a way to dehumanize us, to reduce us to mere objects for their gratification. They gaslight, victim-blame, and minimize the impact of their actions to maintain power and control over their victims (Callahan & Blaine, 2021).

It's important to note that sexual abuse is a serious and traumatic experience and it's never your fault. Regardless of what anyone else might say or how they might make you feel, your experience is still valid even if no one believes you. It doesn't matter if you haven't shared your experience with anyone. It also doesn't matter if you didn't say "no" to them or never said "yes" either.

Your experience is still valid even if you were in a romantic relationship with them. It's still valid if it took you some time to realize that it was a traumatic experience; even if it only affected you at a later stage in life.

Most people will only ever come to understand abuse as something that is beyond physical—something that leaves you blue and black from beatings and lashings. But the thing that makes narcissistic abuse so particularly dangerous is the scars that it leaves hidden away in your soul.

Your internal system literally starts to shut down and break down because you are constantly being lied to. You are constantly being gaslit, controlled, and stripped of your individuality. Sometimes, you don't catch the after-effects for years after you have been subjected to their toxic behavior.

Manipulation for Sport

I've learned a few things after years of being manipulated:

- No matter how kind, generous, or empathetic someone appears to be, you must allow yourself to evaluate that person's behavior based on their current behavior. If their actions don't align with their words, it's time to do a check.

- If you are finding yourself getting more and more confused and are having a tough time trusting your instincts, that is a major red flag. Take some time to reflect and understand what is going on.

- Never let go of your support system. Don't ever let go of the people who validate you and make you feel good about yourself; especially so if someone is placing an unrealistic amount of pressure to let go of the good people in your life.

- Loving, caring, and trusting someone won't necessarily mean that they feel the same way about you. Love is not enough—respect is non-negotiable.

- Even if you love someone unconditionally, it doesn't mean that you have to put up with and take everything that they throw at you.

- When you say no to hurtful behaviors, it doesn't make you mean, rude, or thoughtless. Being able to say no is an indicator of a healthy and thriving relationship. If someone can't take no for an answer, that is a major red flag.

- If the relationship that you have with yourself is starting to suffer because of your relationship with someone else, you may need to start reevaluating the relationship that you have with the person.

Manipulation Defined

Manipulation is being blamed for someone else's toxic behavior that is hardly at all your fault. Narcissists love to test your loyalty. This will happen a lot where they create a situation and see if you will then pick their side. Most of the time, it's going to be one of the prettiest things that there can be (Firestone, 2019).

They have their own definition of what loyalty is, and it's subject to change over what they are feeling and what their mood is for that day. So, when you don't pick their side, they are going to make you feel guilty about it and make a big fat deal out of it. A manipulator often appears as follows:

- They are overly charming.

- They are an expert liar.

- They will, at any cost, use the silent treatment to get their way.

- They will isolate you from others.

- They will make you question your sanity and reality.

- They never accept the blame.

- They seek out emotionally vulnerable people.

- The guilt trip and gaslight people.

- They are petty and passive-aggressive.

- They make fun of and judge you.

How They Manipulate You

The narcissist's manipulative process is often complex, yet subtle, but certain behaviors are part of their process. Let's take a look at what they are:

- **They position themselves as an intellectually superior being.** They will, at any point, do anything they can to invalidate you or your points of view. My former narcissistic partner's favorite response to anything that I would say used to be this: "Oh, but you do know that there is more to the concept than that, don't you? Most times as well, even if they chip at what you say, they will simply change the subject as if what you said doesn't matter at all.

- **They dominate.** Here is something that my partner used to also say to me regularly: "Oh, but these glasses in the cupboard have scuff marks. It's not rocket science to polish a glass properly." They're full of themselves and they experience some kind of a high when they bring other people down.

- **They want to be put on a pedestal.** They want to be revered, and sometimes even feared. "I'm superior because I have achieved [X, Y, & Z]." And most of the time, they won't do things out of the goodness of their hearts, but because they want to be considered "important." They want to come across as a "savior" and when they do something for you, they won't make you forget it.

- **They violate your boundaries.** This is done without shame because it brings them a certain kind of thrill. We'll discuss this some more below.

Boundaries

Relationships thrive when there are healthy boundaries between the partners. You don't have to give all of yourself to that person because you'll end up not liking what you're left with.

We set boundaries to accommodate our needs. We don't set them because we don't value someone or because we don't love them. We don't set boundaries to show spite. We don't set them because of the other person; we set them for ourselves and because we love and mean that much to ourselves.

We hold and maintain our boundaries so that we can show up as the very best versions of ourselves. Some people will never be able to respect that, and you should never for a second think that it is about you. If we want boundaries to work, we must communicate them from a place that says, "I'm doing this because I want to give you the very best of what I can give you."

Healthy relationship boundaries are about being able to establish expectations around finances and how you both are going to manage them. We all grew up with different financial situations, so we all have our own feelings and perceptions about money. We should know our partner's money management style and vice versa.

You should be able to discuss expectations around physical intimacy. It's important that you and your partner feel safe and seen in each other's intimacy.

Respecting each other's time and personal space is an indicator of healthy and strong boundaries. Your partner should know your preferences for personal space and you should know theirs as well. We can't be with someone 24/7 and still manage to be our best selves, no matter how compatible we may seem.

You should both be able to agree on how conflicts are going to be resolved healthily and constructively. You should be able to communicate when you think they have crossed a line. There are parts of us that need a little bit of healing, so that means that something that seems meaningless to them might be the very thing that triggers deep hurt within us.

Healthy relationship boundaries look like having the freedom to freely say and express these things:

- "I don't feel loved or safe when you talk to me in that way."

- "I get annoyed or it upsets me when you talk over me and dismiss what I have to say."

- "Change is hard, but I'm not going to wait around for you to change your behaviors."

- "I can't hear you speak when you shout."

Remember, relationships aren't just about unconditional love. We have to work hard for that stability and passion that we want, but sadly, the narcissistic partner doesn't understand this.

Narcissistic partners will, at any available opportunity, violate both your physical and emotional boundaries to maintain control and power over the relationship. This is how they do it:

- **Disrespecting your physical boundaries.** They will ignore your requests for personal space or physical intimacy or push you to engage in sexual acts that you are uncomfortable with. They may also invade your personal space by going through your belongings, following you without your consent, or showing up to places you've gone to unannounced.

- **Disrespecting your emotional boundaries.** They will invalidate your feelings, belittle your opinions, or gaslight you by denying your perception of reality. They may also manipulate your emotions by using guilt, fear, or anger to control your behavior or make you feel responsible for their needs.

- **Controlling your behavior.** They want to have a say over everything you say, wear, or do by criticizing your choices, setting unrealistic expectations, or punishing you for not complying with their demands. They may also isolate you from your friends and family, or try to control your finances and other resources.

- **Violating your trust.** A narcissistic partner will lie to you, cheat on you, or betray your confidence to maintain their own sense of superiority or entitlement. They will also go as far as to use your vulnerabilities or secrets against you or threaten to expose them to others.

A narcissistic partner doesn't respect you, so they will violate your boundaries in various ways, in ways that are harmful to your well-being and self-esteem.

What to Do When Boundaries Are Violated

Dealing with a narcissistic partner who violates your boundaries is particularly challenging and not an easy situation to navigate. Here are some tips that can help you move toward healthy healing.

- **Recognize the signs of narcissism.** We've established that narcissists often have an exaggerated sense of self-importance, a lack of empathy, and a need for admiration. They may manipulate and exploit you to meet their own needs.

- **Be firm and assertive.** As hard as it might be for you, you have to learn to stand your ground. When a narcissistic partner violates your boundaries, it is important to be clear and direct in your communication. Be firm in your stance and assertive in your tone, but avoid reacting emotionally or engaging in arguments. Here are five statements that you can use as your go-to when a partner challenges your boundaries:

  o "We do have differing opinions about this, but I'm not going to argue about something that feels right and true to me."

- o "I have thought long and hard about this, and still, my position remains as firm as it initially was."

- o "You don't have to agree with my perspective, but what I would like you to do is respect it please."

- o "I've changed a lot since we met, and that means that my needs will be different now."

- o "Please don't talk to me that way. My tolerance for being treated or being spoken to that way has changed."

- **Set realistic expectations.** It's important to recognize that a narcissistic person may not be capable of changing their behavior, even if they promise to do so. Set realistic expectations and prepare yourself for what you can expect from them. Be prepared to enforce consequences if they continue to violate your boundaries.

- **Seek support.** Talk to a therapist or counselor. Being in a relationship with a narcissist is an incredibly isolating experience. Talking to a professional can help you gain a clearer perspective and you will also have the support that you need to deal with the behavior of your narcissistic partner.

- **Maybe it's time to leave.** Narcissists won't change, or let's rather say, you can't change a person who doesn't want to change themselves. This is a difficult decision, but, ultimately, you have to remember that sacrificing your physical and mental health is not worth it. Always remember that if someone attempts to control you all the time, through fear tactics or threats or anything of that kind, it isn't love.

Ways to Deal With a Manipulative Partner

I always say that when you have a good relationship with yourself, then the likelihood of you tolerating poor or demeaning behavior from another is going to be a little less likely. That is because of all the healed and unhealed parts that make you more magnified, and despite what you've been through, it is possible to heal and nurture that relationship with yourself. Believe me, it is!

But, before we get into that, we are going to unpack how we can learn to deal with a narcissistic partner's manipulative ways:

- **Listen to your inner voice/gut intuition.** Or whatever you would like to call it. It never lies. If you feel that your partners' behavior is intrusive/abusive/ aggressive. Then it is. Subconsciously, we all know how we want to and deserve to be treated, so if the way your partner treats you doesn't feel right to you, then it's certainly not right.

   When you feel that they are trying to strip away from you of your power of choice, you have to start being extra firm and clear about your choices. Communicating with a narcissistic partner is hardly a walk in the park, but it's important to be firm and clear when setting boundaries and expressing your needs. Here are some tips:

- **Be clear and direct.** Narcissistic people often try to manipulate or twist your words to suit their needs. To avoid this, be clear and straightforward in your communication. Use "I" statements to express and validate your feelings and needs, and avoid accusing or blaming language.

- **Stick to the facts.** Narcissists will often try to deflect or deny responsibility for their actions. Stick to the facts and avoid getting sidetracked by their attempts to manipulate or twist the conversation.

- **Set boundaries.** Narcissists often feel entitled and may try to push your boundaries. Be firm in setting and enforcing your boundaries; don't be afraid to say no when necessary.

- **Don't engage in arguments.** Narcissists, in some sick and twisted way, want you to pick a fight with them because that is going to allow them to assert their dominance or deflect from the real issue. Don't engage in these arguments; instead, focus on the issue at hand.

- **Take care of yourself.** Dealing with a narcissistic partner is emotionally draining. Take care of yourself by setting aside time to focus on self-care. Make sure you seek support from friends, family, or a therapist if needed.

Remember that you can't change a narcissistic partner, but do you know that you have the power to change and control? By being firm and clear in your communication and setting boundaries, you can protect yourself and maintain the self-respect you have for yourself.

Understand the essential and fundamental rights that you have as a human being:

- o You have a divine right to be treated with respect.

- o You have a right to be able to express your feelings and opinions without having them pushed aside or minimized by another.

- o You have a right to set out and lay out your priorities.

- o You have a right to say no without feeling guilty.

- o You have a right to say no to things without having to explain yourself.

- o You are allowed to protect yourself if you feel like someone is threatening you emotionally or physically.

- o You are allowed to create a healthy and joyful life for yourself.

When you know what your rights are and how you as a human deserve to be treated, you're going to be able to protect yourself from the sick and twisted psychological tactics that the narcissist wants to impose on you.

- **Try not to give in to self-blame.** It's not your fault, even if that is what your manipulative partner wants you to believe.

Understandably, you may feel inadequate and, therefore, place all of that blame upon yourself, but remember that you are not the problem, you are simply being manipulated and getting coerced into believing that it is, in fact, your fault. So, in those moments of blame, turn inward and remember to ask yourself these questions:

- o Am I being treated with the respect that I deserve?

- o Does this person have unreasonable and unrealistic expectations of me?

- o Is the relationship a two-way street or is it simply just a one-sided affair where I'm being shut out and dismissed all the time?

- o Is this relationship making me feel good about myself or am I simply just second-guessing myself all of the time?

- **Ask them questions.** So, your manipulator makes unreasonable requests of you because they want you to go out of your way for them. So, sometimes when you get an unreasonable request from them, it can be helpful to shift the attention back to them by asking them questions and waiting for their response. For example:

  - o "Doesn't this sound a bit unreasonable to you?"

  - o "Do you think that what you're asking of me sounds fair?"

  - o "Are you asking me or are you telling me to do this?"

  - o "Do you just expect me to do this without saying anything about how I feel about it?"

Reclaiming Yourself After Being Manipulated

Coming back to yourself after experiencing manipulation can be a challenging and complex process. Here are some steps that might help:

- **Acknowledge what has happened.** It happened to you. Recognize that you have been manipulated and that it has impacted your sense of self. It's important to validate your experience and understand that it's normal to feel confused or uncertain about who you are.

- **Find a good support system.** Find people you trust and feel comfortable talking to, such as friends, family members, or a therapist. Sharing your experience with others can help you process your emotions and gain perspective on what has happened. Always remember that in sharing our experiences with others, we will feel less alone.

- **Reflect on your values and beliefs**. Take some time to reflect on what's important to you and what you believe in. This can help you reconnect with your sense of self and identify the qualities that define who you are.

- **Practice self-care.** Immerse yourself in activities that promote self-care and self-compassion. They don't have to be big things. Simple things such as exercise, meditation, or spending time in nature will work perfectly. This can help you feel more grounded and connected to yourself.

The one reminder and thought that I hold on dearly to is this: Just because someone didn't love you like you deserved to be loved and didn't treat you like you deserved to be treated, it doesn't mean that everyone you encounter will treat you that way. How you were treated is not a reflection on you—it's on them. You deserve love, kindness, and consideration in abundance.

Chapter 3:

Fighting the Urge...

How we feel about our emotions has a major impact on how we cope and how long those emotions last. When I used to feel guilty about leaving my partner, I would experience so much frustration and fear about that guilt that emerged. "But I shouldn't be feeling guilty about this," I would scream at myself. "I know that this was a healthy and important thing to do for myself and my mental health, so why do I feel like this?"

This guilt, in not so many ways, signified that I must've done something wrong, "something bad," because if not, why else would it be there? But now, I have come to learn what I can do to reframe that guilt. I think of it as a kind of growing pain. Like that soreness that you experience after a good ole workout. That guilt that I feel after expressing my needs or leaving situations that aren't healthy is a sign that I have been working out and doing so really hard.

The less I exercise that muscle, the stronger the pain or the guilt will be, but the more I exercise and put those muscles to good use, the less painful the guilt becomes. It's important that we assign meaning to it and this is why: Knowing that the guilt will be there makes us anticipate it so that it doesn't catch us off guard when it decides to finally make an appearance. Secondly, it gives us a resilient spirit. It helps us to approach our guilt from a place of compassion rather than hate; thus, making it more bearable and quicker to overcome.

But why do we experience guilt, even when we know that we are doing the right and best thing for ourselves? Well, firstly, we feel guilty because we have made a significant investment of time, emotions, and energy in the relationship. All of the times when you stayed for the sake of making things work, you bent over backward for them and sacrificed so much. Leaving the relationship makes you feel like a failure or a waste. That's why we blame ourselves: Because, despite all our best efforts and intentions, we failed to make a "good thing work."

Secondly, we feel guilty because we fear the other person's reaction. In toxic relationships, there may be a pattern of manipulation, control, or even abuse. So, we often don't know how that narcissistic partner will react. Would their reaction mean the end of your life? These are very real questions that we grapple with. So, sometimes, the best and only option that we seem to think we have is to stay and hope that things will get better.

And finally, we experience a sense of guilt because we have been conditioned to believe that the problems in the relationship are our fault.

My partner used to say to me, "I'm doing this because I love you." No. That was them basically trying to justify their mistreatment.

"It's no wonder nobody likes you all that much," as an attempt to destroy any self-worth that I had.

And more:

- "You're overreacting. You always blow things out of proportion."

- "If you would just do what I say, we wouldn't have these problems."

- "I wouldn't have to treat you this way if you weren't so difficult."

- "You're too sensitive. You need to toughen up."

- "You're the one who started this argument."

- "I was joking. Why can't you take a joke?"

- "You're so selfish. All you care about is yourself."

- "If you really loved me, you would do what I want."

- "I don't know why I put up with you. You're impossible to deal with."

- "You're making a big deal out of nothing. It's not that serious."

Toxic relationships involve a power dynamic where one person tries to control and manipulate the other. You come to believe that you are responsible for the problems in the relationship, and that leads to feelings of guilt and shame.

The Urge to Feel Guilty for Leaving

You are allowed and have a full session to stand up for yourself, your strength, and all of your brilliant self. If someone else can't or fails to honor you where you deserve to be honored, you are allowed to carry on and build a new life wholly without them. The first step in overcoming that guilt that comes from letting go and starting over is realizing and accepting that feeling guilty is a normal and understandable response to leaving a toxic relationship.

Leaving a toxic relationship can be a challenging, emotional, and gut-wrenching process. It's normal to experience guilt or feel conflicted about your decision. Below are some tips that may help you overcome those feelings of guilt.

Recognize That Your Well-Being Is Important

It's important to remember that you deserve to be in a healthy and positive relationship. Putting your own well-being first isn't selfish; it's necessary. When it's hard or when you feel most tempted to go back to them, remind yourself that you can't possibly fix everything or be everything that that toxic person wants you to be to them. The freedom that you need and so desperately desire is waiting for you on the other side of leaving and letting go. Repeat this mantra as well:

"I'm choosing to release my energy from the situations and people who are draining me and robbing me of my identity. I may not be able to immediately change these circumstances and situations, but I'll certainly stop feeding into this constant stream and overflow of negativity. I'm choosing myself."

Seek Support From Loved Ones

Talk to trusted friends and family members about your decision to leave the toxic relationship. They can offer emotional support and help you stay on track. Going through tough situations alone is not and should not be an option for you. People who love and truly care about us can offer a platform for us to share our feelings—a platform where judgment doesn't exist. To the right people, you'll never be too much or feel like a burden.

Practice Self-Care

Engage in activities that make you feel good, whether it's exercise, spending time in nature, or indulging in a hobby. Taking care of yourself can help you feel more confident and in control. Show up for yourself. If you are wondering and asking yourself what it is that you can do to show that, here are some ideas:

- Get in the habit of regularly asking yourself, *What do my heart and soul need from me today?*

- Check in with yourself and be completely honest.

- Listen and honor your emotions and feelings without judgment.

- Speak to yourself kindly.

- Do something for our body, mind, or soul—a mani-pedi, a walk outside, visits to the library, creating art, watching your favorite shows, going for a facial, or a day where you sit and do nothing. Sounds like great ideas, don't you think?

- Instead of comparison, focus on gratitude.

- Ask yourself before doing something, *Does this serve me?*

Focus on the Future

Visualize the life you want and think about the opportunities and possibilities that await you. Grab a notebook and write down your dreams for the future. Bring your dreams to life by creating a vision board. You can do this digitally with tools such as Canva, or by using physical resources such as cutouts from magazines or items found in nature. Have you always wanted to improve your culinary skills? A great first step might be to Google free or inexpensive cooking classes near you.

What are some other things that you have wanted to try but have held yourself back for one reason or another? Is it spoken word poetry? Look for open mic nights in your area, join local writing groups, or join a Facebook community for aspiring poets. Regardless of your aspirations for the future, initiating small actions toward them is the ideal approach and something you can begin today! Step out there and reach for the stars. You are 100% worthy and deserving of all the beauty this world has to offer!

I hope that you never forget that leaving isn't a sign of failure. It's a symbol of strength and a bold declaration of love from yourself to yourself. Some people will never truly understand what accountability is. Letting go and choosing to put yourself first is what will help you move forward and closer to the kind of love that you truly do deserve. And remember that you can always try to make your life a little bit better in the smallest and simplest of ways, and as long as you are trying, you can hold on to the reminder that you truly are going to be okay.

The Urge to Self-Blame

Self-blame offers us the illusion that we could've changed the outcome; that if we had given in and said yes, instead of saying no; that if we had changed our boundaries to suit the needs of our narcissistic partners, none of that would've happened. It allows us to momentarily believe that we have more power than we actually do, and in some way, it offers us some hope, rather than despair.

This is because when you're using self-blame, you are essentially telling yourself that you are responsible for how your partner behaved, so when the outcome feels like it's a bad one, your mind will work hard at trying to offer you a solution to "fix" the problem, and that more often than not, will show up in the form of self-blame.

If you, for example, need solitude and personal space, you will have to prepare for your partner's reaction. So, if your narcissistic partner has gotten accustomed to you always accommodating their needs, by you changing and being unavailable, it will be perceived as a personal attack on them. Because they have poor interpersonal skills and almost no self-regulation skills, they will communicate their feelings in a passive-aggressive manner, or by making you feel like you're the biggest prick on the planet.

You might be reading this and thinking to yourself, *But isn't this the same as guilt then?* No. Self-blame and guilt are related, but they're not the same.

Self-blame refers to the act of holding yourself accountable for something that has gone wrong or a mistake that has been made, even when you may not be fully or solely responsible. It can also refer to feeling responsible for the actions or feelings of others, even when these are beyond your control.

Guilt, on the other hand, is an emotional response to a specific action or behavior that is perceived as wrong or harmful; either by yourself or others. Guilt can be a healthy emotion only if it leads to taking responsibility for your actions, making amends or reparations, and learning from the experience to make better choices in the future. However, excessive or irrational guilt can lead to feelings of shame, self-doubt, and distress.

In narcissistic relationships, self-blame can be a common experience as your narcissistic partner may use manipulation and gaslighting to make you feel responsible for problems in the relationship. This can lead to feelings of guilt, but it is important to recognize that these feelings are not necessarily justified and may be a result of the dynamics of the relationship.

Disengaging From Self-Blame

Invite a little bit more tenderness into your life. You deserve the whole lot of it. Am I saying that it's going to be easy to stop blaming yourself? Nope. Overcoming self-blame is a process and it also requires time and an emotional investment. But with time, patience, and self-compassion, you can and will get to the side of a happier you: the part where you get to reclaim the whole of who you are.

Here are some tips that can come in handy for you:

- **Recognize that self-blame is a common reaction.** It's natural to feel responsible for things that happen to us or others, even when we have little or no control over the situation. Recognizing this can help you understand that self-blame is a common reaction and not a reflection of your failure.

- **Challenge your negative thoughts.** Often, our self-blame is fueled by negative thoughts and beliefs about ourselves. Challenge these thoughts by asking yourself if they are rational and if there is evidence to support them. Reframe the negative thoughts into more balanced, positive, and affirming thoughts. Here are some questions that can help challenge negative self-blaming thoughts:

  o What evidence do I have that supports my self-blaming thought?

- Am I being too hard on myself?

- Would I think the same way about someone else in my situation?

- Am I taking responsibility for things outside of my control?

- What other factors could have contributed to the situation, aside from my actions?

- How would I advise a friend who had the same self-blaming thought?

- Is there another way to interpret the situation that doesn't involve blaming myself?

- What can I learn from this situation, regardless of who is at fault?

- What are some positive things I have done in the past that contradict my self-blaming thoughts?

- Am I giving myself credit for the things that went well, or only focusing on the negative aspects?

- **Practice self-compassion.** Self-compassionate people say:

  - "I trust that I can deal with difficult feelings."

  - "I can extend the same love and kindness that I extend to others."

  - "I deserve to give myself the same amount of grace, understanding, and kindness that I so freely give to others."

  - "I can allow things to unfold without self-judgment."

  - "I'm allowed to be patient with myself as I figure things out."

Treat yourself with the same kindness and understanding that you would offer to a good friend who is going through a tough time. Acknowledge your pain and suffering, and offer yourself words of comfort and support.

Use affirmations to motivate and guide you whenever you feel like you are being a little too hard on yourself. Some of my favorites are these:

- o "I'm choosing to let go of the illusion that I'm supposed to be perfect all the time. I'm allowing myself to be human and to experience emotions as I should."

- o "I'm forgiving myself for all of those times when I didn't know better. I'm choosing to celebrate the progress that I'm making."

- o "I'm trusting my timeline. It doesn't matter how much time it takes me to heal; all that matters is that I'm working on myself."

- o "At any moment or time, I have the power to make new choices that propel me in a new direction. In choosing to let go, I'm doing just that."

- o "I'm working on myself so that I can become the very best version of myself. I'm choosing to love myself in the way that I desire to be loved. I deserve to prioritize my well-being."

- **Be mindful of your thoughts and emotions.** Notice and acknowledge when you are feeling anxious, stressed, or overwhelmed, and allow yourself to feel these emotions without judgment.

- **Treat yourself with kindness.** We can't heal when we are constantly being critical of ourselves. We can't heal when resentment is at the forefront. Speak to yourself compassionately and supportively, just as you would to a good friend who is going through a tough time.

- **Take care of your physical and emotional needs.** Do this by eating well, getting enough sleep, exercising, and engaging in activities that bring you joy and relaxation. A healthy and happy body equals a healthy state of mind; believe me, this is true.

- **Practice gratitude.** Gratitude is lived out in the present moment, not in daydreams. Focus on the positive things in your life, and take time to appreciate and be grateful for them. I've found that when I look at life from a place of contentment and gratitude, things feel a lot easier. They become a lot better. And by gratitude, I don't mean that I focus on the big extraordinary moments, no.

  It's about taking pride and pleasure in the small moments that on any other day would seem so insignificant. I don't want to wish away the goodness of the moment. Here are some helpful tips for you to help you practice gratitude when gratitude seems far:

    - **Keep a gratitude journal.** Believe me, this works. Carve out a few minutes each day to write down three things you are grateful for. This can be as simple as enjoying a warm cup of coffee or spending time with your closest family and friends.

    - **Express gratitude to others.** "Thank you." Those are two words that drastically transformed my relationships with my people. "Thank you for your time." "Thank you for the help that you offered." "Thank you for being you." "Thank you for accepting me as I am." Take the time to thank those around you for their contributions, whether it's a coworker who helped you with a project or a friend who listened to you vent.

    - **Live here in the moment.** Instead of getting caught up in what you don't have, focus on what you do have in the present moment. Appreciate the small things that bring you joy, such as a beautiful sunset or a delicious meal.

- **Practice mindfulness.** Incorporate mindfulness practices into your daily routine, such as meditation or deep breathing exercises. This can help you focus on the present moment and cultivate a sense of gratitude.

Take a few minutes out of your day to reflect on the tiny magnificent experiences of your life—the moments that brought you an inexplicable amount of joy in your life. In doing this, you are shifting the focus from the "lack" to the abundance and sufficiency in your life. When you appreciate the good things in your life, you will be inspired to be more grateful for both the big and small things.

- **Practice self-forgiveness.** Self-forgiveness is one of the most challenging aspects of reclaiming and finding your voice after having been in a narcissistic relationship. It's a lot easier to give and extend grace to other people in their time of need, but to do that same thing for ourselves is not all that easy. But the one thing that I know is true is that healing starts when we stop blaming ourselves for all of the things that we went through.

So, forgive yourself for past mistakes and shortcomings, and let go of self-criticism and negative self-talk. If you don't know where or how to even start, this is how you can do it:

  - **Acknowledge the abuse.** Your experience is a valid one. Recognize that you are a victim of narcissistic abuse. It's important to understand that the abuse was not your fault and that you didn't deserve it.

  - **Educate yourself.** There are no shortages of resources that inform us about the effects and behaviors of narcissistic partners. Teach yourself about narcissism and narcissistic abuse and the effects they can have on individuals. Understanding how and why the abuse happened can help you make sense of what happened and begin your journey to healing.

  - **Set boundaries.** Set healthy boundaries with the narcissist and anyone else who may not respect your needs and boundaries. This can help you regain a sense of control and self-respect.

- o **Focus on the strengths and qualities that make you unique and valuable.** Building your self-esteem and confidence will help you move forward and overcome the harmful effects of the abuse. Also having things that you are passionate and focused on sprinkles a whole lot of meaning and purpose to love, and that will help you move forward and to infuse more enjoyment into your life.

Practice self-forgiveness by accepting responsibility for any choices you made that may have contributed to the situation, but also recognizing that you were in a difficult and abusive situation. Remember that forgiveness is a process, and it may take time to fully let go of any negative self-talk.

Here are 10 self-forgiveness mantras or affirmations that you can also use to help you practice self-forgiveness:

- o "I forgive myself for any mistakes I have made in the past, and I release any negative feelings I have toward myself."

- o "I'm worthy of love, compassion, and forgiveness, and I give myself permission to let go of any self-blame or self-judgment."

- o "I accept myself for who I am, flaws and all, and I trust that I'm doing the best I can in every moment."

- o "I'm not defined by my mistakes and I choose to learn from them and grow as a person."

- o "I'm deserving of my own forgiveness, and I allow myself to move forward with a sense of peace and acceptance."

- o "I acknowledge my past mistakes, but I choose to focus on the present moment and the positive changes I can make in my life."

- o "I let go of any negative self-talk or limiting beliefs that hold me back, and I choose to embrace self-love and self-compassion."

- o "I'm a work in progress, and I give myself permission to make mistakes and learn from them."

- o "I release any guilt, shame, or regret that I may be holding onto, and I choose to move forward with a sense of forgiveness and compassion toward myself."

- o "I'm grateful for the opportunity to practice self-forgiveness, and I trust that it will lead me to greater peace, happiness, and fulfillment."

- **Take responsibility for what you can control.** While it's important to recognize that some situations are beyond our control, there may be aspects of the situation that we can take responsibility for. Focus on what you can control and take action to make positive changes.

The Urge to Apologize to Them

If you are in a relationship with a narcissist, then you are certainly no stranger to over-apologizing. Over-apologizing to a narcissist can take many forms, shows up in a variety of ways, and may involve apologizing for things that are not your fault or that are minor. Here are some examples of what over-apologizing looks like:

- **Apologizing for their behavior.** If your partner has behaved badly, such as yelling at you or insulting you, you may feel compelled to apologize to them to avoid conflict or to placate them.

- **Apologizing for your feelings.** If your partner dismisses or belittles your feelings, you may feel like you need to apologize for having them. For example, you may apologize for being upset or for expressing your frustration.

- **Apologizing for things that are not your fault.** They blame others for their mistakes or shortcomings. You may find yourself apologizing for things that are outside of your control or that are not your responsibility.

- **Apologizing excessively.** You may feel like you need to apologize repeatedly for the same issue, even if you have already apologized multiple times. This can be a sign that you are trying to appease your partner or to make up for something that was not your fault.

- **Apologizing for not meeting their expectations.** Narcissists can have very high expectations of others and may become angry or upset if those expectations are not met. You may feel like you need to apologize for not living up to their standards, even if those standards are unrealistic or unreasonable.

We over-apologize for a variety of reasons. Some of the reasons why we feel the need to apologize to a narcissistic partner include:

  o **Fear of their reaction.** Narcissists are, in some way, a plain and simple definition of what a ticking time bomb is because they are very sensitive to criticism and may react with anger, hostility, or even violence. They are sensitive to criticism because they have an inflated sense of self-importance and a deep-seated need for admiration and validation from others. They see themselves as superior and believe that they are entitled to special treatment and recognition.

  When they receive criticism, it can be perceived as a threat and an attack on their self-image, and this challenges their grandiose sense of self.

They also often cannot take responsibility for their own mistakes or shortcomings, and may instead blame others or external factors for their failures. Criticism can be seen as further evidence of their perceived inadequacy, which can be deeply threatening to their fragile self-esteem. So, in an attempt to avoid their explosive reaction, you over-apologize just to protect yourself from their toxic reaction.

o **Guilt.** We've established that narcissists are often skilled at making others feel guilty for things that are not their fault because they may manipulate you into feeling responsible for their behavior, leading you to apologize even when you have done nothing wrong.

o **Desire for approval.** They are charming and charismatic and know which of your buttons to press, and it can be easy to become emotionally dependent on their approval and praise. Apologizing may be a way to seek their approval and maintain the relationship.

o **Gaslighting.** Narcissists may use gaslighting to make you doubt your own perceptions and beliefs. They may tell you that you are overreacting or imagining things, leading you to apologize for your feelings or actions.

o **Need for peace.** Sometimes, the only way to find peace is to be the peacemaker. Narcissists are demanding and may create a lot of conflict in the relationship. Apologizing may be a way to defuse the situation and restore peace, even if you do not believe you have done anything wrong.

Practical Steps When You Really Feel Like Apologizing

Imagine that you are a flower that is seeking to thrive and grow to your fullest potential. You need sunlight, water, and some nutrients to bloom into a beautiful, healthy plant. Now, imagine that your narcissistic partner is a parasitic weed, latching onto you—draining you of your vitality. This is the weed that takes all of your sunlight, water, and nutrients, leaving you weak and wilted.

To thrive and grow, you can't occupy the same space as the weed. It is essential for your recovery and well-being. Only then will you begin to nourish yourself and take the steps necessary to become the beautiful, healthy flower you were meant to be.

Cutting off contact with a narcissistic partner is like removing the parasitic weed from your life. It may be a painful process, but it is necessary to reclaim your power and regain control of your life. Like the flower, you will begin to bloom and flourish once you rid yourself of the toxic influence of the narcissistic partner.

Over-apologizing is somewhat addictive, I tell you. But the one thing that my therapist taught me is that it's actually reassurance-seeking. It's also an attempt to bolster our doubts by seeking validation from others. It's relieving in the short run, but when we're thinking about the long term, it's not sustainable, nor is it healthy.

I want us to start this chapter with a little bit of love. We're going to practice mantras that you can use to reground and regroup yourself when that urge to over-apologize becomes too strong:

- "I'm worthy of respect and love."

- "I will no longer apologize for things I'm not responsible for."

- "I trust that the decision I've made to leave is the right one for me."

- "I'm strong enough to overcome the urge to apologize unnecessarily."

- "I'm deserving of happiness and positivity in my life."

- "I'm capable of making sound decisions for my own well-being."

- "I will prioritize my mental and emotional health above all else."

- "I'm not responsible for the actions or emotions of others."

- "I trust myself to set healthy boundaries and stick to them."

- "I'm valuable and deserving of a healthy, positive relationship."

- "I'm aware of my worth and won't settle for less; only those who treat me with respect deserve to have access to me."

- "I have all the power within me to make positive changes in my life."

- "I'm not defined by my past experiences."

- "I'm confident in myself and my abilities."

- "I won't allow anyone to make me feel less than I am."

- "I'm capable of forgiving myself for past mistakes and moving forward."

- "I will no longer dwell on negativity or toxicity."

- "I'm worthy of respect and won't tolerate disrespect in any form."

- "I'm focusing on healing and building a positive future for myself."

- "I'm grateful for the strength and resilience I possess."

You don't owe anyone an apology for the things that you didn't do or things that aren't your fault. You don't owe anyone an explanation about your appearance or your values. You don't have to apologize for not having the answers to everything. You don't have to apologize for things that other grown adults do. Read this for as many times as you want. It also took me quite some time to accept it as a truth.

Apologizing to a narcissist can be challenging, as they may not be receptive to the apology and may even use it as an opportunity to manipulate further or control the situation. However, if you feel a strong desire to apologize to a narcissist, here are some practical steps you can take:

1. **Take a step back and reflect on your motivations.** This part here is all about awareness—the first step to making the change that you want. Why do you feel the need to apologize? Did you do something wrong? Are you taking responsibility for something that is their fault and not your own? If you believe that you did do something wrong, you can always check in with someone else to get their perspective on the situation. We judge ourselves too harshly; thus, are unfair to ourselves in most situations.

2. **Consider the potential outcomes of apologizing.** Is the apology going to make things better in any way? Will it help to repair the relationship or improve the situation? Or, will it simply provide the narcissist with more ammunition to use against you?

3. **Set boundaries and expectations for future interactions.** Let the narcissist know what you are willing and unwilling to tolerate, and communicate any consequences for violating those boundaries.

4. **Practice self-care and prioritize your own well-being.** Dealing with a narcissist can be emotionally draining and exhausting, so make sure to take care of yourself and seek support from trusted friends, family members, or professionals if needed.

The damage that over-apologizing does to you is detrimental. Constantly abandoning yourself is preventing you from having a clear sense of self from which you derive your needs and values;

understanding your needs is how you develop a strong sense of self and thrive in the way that you were meant to be.

The Urge to Go Back to Them

My therapist told me once that we usually gravitate toward what feels familiar to us. So, if one-sided and toxic relationships are all you've ever known, you'll be tempted. And if the love of a narcissist is the only kind of love that you'd gotten used to, you're going to want to go back to them. Experiencing urges to go back to toxic relationships is a common experience for many people who have been in such relationships. Some of the reasons include:

- **Familiarity.** As mentioned, even if a relationship is toxic, it can be familiar and comfortable, especially if it has been a long-term one. When we are used to a certain dynamic, it can be hard to break away from it, even if we know it isn't healthy.

- **Fear of the unknown.** Leaving a toxic relationship can be scary because it means facing the unknown and stepping outside of our comfort zone. "Rather a familiar hell than an unknown heaven" is the expression that would be the best to describe this situation. I mean, the only life that you've ever known is one with abuse. You're going to feel apprehensive at the thought of starting a new and fresh life without them. That fear of being alone or not finding someone else can make us want to stay in that familiar misery, even if it's unhealthy for us.

  It's important to remember that leaving a toxic relationship is a process, and it's not always easy. Recognizing your worth and the value that you hold as a human being is essential to helping you break away from that toxic cycle of leaving and returning to them. This involves understanding and acknowledging the strengths that you have as a human.

  This awareness is what'll help you build solid self-esteem and give you the courage that you need to leave and start setting healthy boundaries, and the wisdom that you need to make healthier choices when it comes to your relationships.

By being able to recognize your worth and value, you will be able to maintain and build relationships with people who recognize your worth: people who value and respect you and treat you in the way you truly deserve to be treated. And always remember that if you're in a relationship because you're looking for something to take away your pain or loneliness, you aren't looking for love, you're looking for relief. You can't be a partner if you're not taking any responsibility for yourself.

How to Fight the Urge to Return to Them

Here's how you can minimize those urges to return to a toxic partner:

- **Learn how to tend and take care of your needs and your heart first.** Do you know what it is that you need to do to fill and replenish your own cup? Do you know how to make your cup overflow goodness? To be able to live well, love well, or do anything well, we need to know how to source from within so that we can tend to our well-being and truly experience the fullness that human connection has to offer.

- **Learn how to set boundaries.** Now, boundaries are something that we talked a lot about throughout the book, but now, I'm going to give you practical tips and pointers on how you can set them.

  So, I'm going to start by saying that a lot of us struggle with setting boundaries because:

  o   We feel fearful about being rejected.

  o   We don't want to hurt others.

  o   We worry too much about what the other person will think about us.

o   We aren't aware that boundaries are necessary.

o   We grew up in environments where boundaries weren't enforced.

o   Our confidence and self-esteem are an issue for us.

o   We have a fear of abandonment.

o   We've had experiences with people not respecting our boundaries in the past. and that is what is influencing and impacting our abilities to set them now.

- **Identify and understand the boundaries that you need.** Before setting boundaries, it's important to identify what you are and aren't willing to tolerate in your relationship. This includes behaviors, actions, and attitudes that are unacceptable to you. Here are a few additional tips that you can also keep in mind to help you identify the boundaries that you need to set:

  o   **Pay attention to your feelings.** If you often feel uncomfortable, anxious, or unhappy with the way your partner treats you, it may be a sign that you need to establish your boundaries.

  o   **Identify your core values.** It could be things like respect, honesty, trust, loyalty, and communication.

  o   **Beware of red flags.** Red flags can be warning signs that someone may be crossing your boundaries. It could be things like ignoring your feelings, isolating you from your friends and family, or controlling your behavior.

  o   **Trust your gut.** Trusting your intuition is crucial when it comes to setting boundaries. If something feels wrong or uncomfortable, it may be a sign that you need to establish stronger boundaries in your relationship.

- o **Take time to reflect.** It can be beneficial to reflect on your past experiences in relationships and what you learned from them. This can help you identify what kind of boundaries you need in your current relationship.

- **Communicate your boundaries clearly.** To set and enforce those boundaries, you're going to have to express them. Use "I" statements to express your needs and boundaries clearly to your partner. For example:

  - o "I feel hurt when you speak to me in a condescending tone. I need you to speak to me with respect."

  - o "I need space to focus on myself and my own goals."

  - o "I'm not comfortable with the way you've been treating me, and I need time to assess the situation."

  - o "I'm putting my own well-being first and setting boundaries that are necessary for my mental health."

  - o "I can't continue a relationship with someone who constantly invalidates my feelings and experiences."

  - o "I need to take time for myself to heal from the emotional damage caused by our relationship."

  - o "I'm not willing to entertain conversations that are manipulative or emotionally draining."

  - o "I'm not responsible for your emotional well-being, and I can't be your sole source of validation and support."

  - o "I need to reduce communication with you to prioritize my own needs and avoid any unnecessary conflicts."

  - o "I will no longer tolerate any behavior that is disrespectful, demeaning, or abusive."

o "I'm setting firm boundaries to protect myself from any further harm in this relationship."

- **Be assertive.** Don't apologize for your boundaries or let your partner manipulate you into changing them. Be firm and assertive in enforcing your boundaries.

- **Expect pushback, but don't give in.** Narcissistic partners may resist your boundaries and try to manipulate you into changing them. Be prepared for this and stand firm in your decision.

- **Set consequences.** What will you do when that person crosses or violates the boundaries you have established? Make sure that you know exactly what course of action you're going to take when your boundaries are crossed. These could be something like seeking counseling or other appropriate measures.

- **Seek support.** Setting boundaries with a narcissistic partner can be emotionally challenging. You are going to need people around you to remind you that you are doing the best thing for yourself. Seek support from friends, family, or a therapist that will help you stay strong and focused.

- **Don't forget about that self-care!** You must take care of yourself physically, emotionally, and mentally. Make sure you're getting enough rest, eating well, and engaging in activities that make you happy and fulfilled.

In my case, practicing self-care meant taking care of and tending to my anxiety. If you, like me, need a little help navigating and tending to that anxiety, here are a few tips for you.

Practice accepting and validating that part of you that gets anxious; the part of you that is trying to protect your tender heart from judgment, rejection, and abandonment. Tell yourself that:

o "It's okay to feel anxious."

- o "It feels tough, but you're safe right now. It makes sense why you're feeling anxious."

- o "It makes sense that I'm feeling anxious. I'm still new at setting boundaries, so it certainly will feel uncomfortable. Anyone else in my shoes would also feel the same."

- **Attend to your needs with compassion and care.** When anxiety strikes, go ahead and ask yourself, *What is it that I need right now? Is it comfortable? Exercise? A conversation with a friend? Breathwork?* Recognize those needs and take the action that you need.

People won't always respond well to the boundaries that we set and enforce. They will attempt to guilt trip us, inflict pain, or even go so far as to manipulate you—the person who is setting the boundary. But, remember that even if people don't agree with your boundaries, they still can and should treat and address them with respect.

Chapter 4:

Beauty in Healing

Healing sometimes seems like such a far-fetched and unattainable thing. I remember when I was at a point where I thought that I would never reach—a point where I thought that I would forever be in pain and my heart in pieces for all eternity. I wondered and asked myself if I would get those days again when I would laugh and enjoy child-like laughter. Days where I would get to do and live life for me…

I wondered if I would ever get to a point where I was okay… Like truly okay and doing well. Until the day came. It was as if drawing your curtains open to allow those first glimmers of morning sunshine to filter through in a room, something stirred and moved inside of me and I knew that I was going to be OKAY. I smiled the brightest that I ever had in what felt like years. I took one foot and put it in front of the other. And I did the same the following day, and the one after that, and so on, until I got to where I am today.

So, wherever you are in your journey, I hope that you are learning and giving yourself the credit that you deserve. I hope that you are acknowledging and praising yourself for how strong you are, I hope you choose to marvel at that ability to pull yourself out of a sticky situation. Allow these realizations to walk with you and guide you. I hope you never take for granted just how strong and capable you are of pulling through.

You have enough courage to keep moving, growing, and healing—I know you do. So, when you feel weak, please go stand in front of a mirror and whisper to yourself: "You're a warrior, and I'm so proud of you." Allow that to be the reserve of strength that you tap into when you need a pick-me-up.

Healing has been a popular topic lately. In some way, we can even say that it's something that has become glamorized in a sense, and that's what has informed our perception and reality about it. But this book is about honesty, so you and I are going to unpack some of those hard, but necessary truths about healing.

Healing will take longer than we expect: It isn't an overnight process. It can take months or even years to heal from emotional or physical trauma fully. It requires patience, perseverance, and a commitment to self-care.

Healing is not as straightforward as we want it to be. It isn't a straight line, and setbacks and relapses are common. Sometimes, you feel like you've made progress, only to have old wounds resurface. This is a normal part of the healing process, and it's important to be gentle with yourself during these times. Through my own process and journey, I've also learned that you're going to experience a lot more sadness than you do on most days. This is the kind of sadness that simply makes you realize how much you missed out on and how much you unnecessarily sacrificed—and darling, that's okay.

It's okay to feel sad over what happened but remember, you don't have to allow that sadness to consume you. You were a different person then—a person who was still getting to know themselves a little bit better—but now that you do know yourself and what you want out of this life, please promise me that you are going to go out there and live your life to the absolute fullest. You have a second chance to make up for all the bliss and beauty you unintentionally missed.

Healing requires facing difficult emotions. It often involves facing difficult memories that you may have been avoiding or suppressing. To make it to that place of healing, you will have to be willing to look within yourself and become aware of all of those areas inside of you that need healing. You need to be willing to acknowledge and look into what is and isn't working. You must be willing to look deeply into your shadows to find the pain you are suppressing.

You're going to need to have a courageous spirit too. It's a lot easier to pretend that you're not hurting or that you're just "fine," but further down the line, it's going to become a lot more difficult to ignore that emotional storm that's brewing inside of you. Honestly, you can only ignore yourself for so long before those areas that need healing start screaming right at you.

Acknowledge the pain, grief, and sadness that you're feeling. Healing requires a lot of vulnerability and detachment from the ego—open up, dear friend, and you'll thank yourself in the future.

Sometimes, the support of our friends might not be enough, so we might need the help of a therapist. While self-care and support from loved ones can be helpful, sometimes, professional help is necessary to heal from trauma fully. Although well-intentioned, the advice that we sometimes receive from friends and family is not what we need.

Our friends and family love us, so, sometimes, they'll go ahead and say things to us because they think it's what we want to hear. Conversely, a therapist sees things objectively and can tell you what you need to hear compassionately.

Healing is ongoing. It isn't a one-time event. You may still encounter challenges and setbacks even after you've made progress. It's important to continue practicing self-care and seeking support as needed to maintain your progress and continue healing. There have been many occurrences throughout my journey where I thought that I was doing okay, but then something would happen and I would be reminded that actually, I still have a long way to go. Some things and situations still trigger me, and that is a sign that I still have some work to do.

We Are Choosing to Heal

I'm learning...

I'm learning that trusting myself will mean that I have to take action instinctively; I can welcome and accept advice from others, but what matters is listening to what I know is true for me.

I'm learning that If I'm constantly looking for what's next or what's better, I'm going to miss out on all the spectacular moments of now.

I'm learning that even in the middle of a mess, I can still be kind and gentle with myself.

Sometimes, I don't want to put in the work that needs to be put in to heal. Sometimes, healing hurts as much as the situation that puts us in that emotional state. It's the equivalent of going to war, but you know what? Despite all the pain and grief that the process comes with, I would still choose myself over and over again in a heartbeat—that's without a doubt.

But despite the process being such a beautiful thing and all, what makes it so hard?

We have been betrayed one too many times and that causes us to lose trust in others. In a toxic relationship, there may be a betrayal or loss of trust over time. This makes it difficult for us to trust others in the future, which can impact our ability to build healthy and thriving relationships with people who are capable of loving and treating us well. You see, when we experience trauma, we often hold on to it as a way of preventing it from happening to us again.

One of the other reasons why it's so difficult is the meaning that we tie to our trauma. We often associate meaning with positive experiences, but as heavy as they are, traumatic experiences also have meanings of their own. The one expression that I love to use to help me understand my experiences and relate them to the world around me is this: "The more meaningful it is to me, the bigger the feelings will be." When it comes to toxic relationships, traumatic experiences, or anything of that kind, the fact that we think about them and grieve just a little shows just how much they meant to us. That relationship was essentially a big part of your life and to just up and forget about it like that isn't easy.

We are under the impression or believe that our trauma is something that we will "get over" some time. Sometimes, we fool ourselves into believing that we're okay; that we've moved on. But the actual truth is that trauma is still very much with us and present in our day-to-day experiences because we are failing to acknowledge what happened.

A comforting reminder that we can all hold on to is that healing is possible for all of us to heal, and oh, you won't have to put your whole life on pause just to get to that place where you're okay. You don't have to rush yourself—you have plenty of time. Embrace the change and transformation that takes place. It's the best and most beautiful part of the process.

Steps to Healing

To heal is to accept and embrace and extend love to every part of our human experience—the ups and downs, the mess, and in-between (especially those). Here are practical steps and tips for you to help you navigate your journey:

- **Learn to accept your feelings as they come.** You can't work through what you're trying to avoid, so that means that you're going to have to have to acknowledge and embrace your emotions for what they are, don't try to suppress or downplay them, so if you're feeling angry, feel it and let it show you what you need to see—most of the time, our anger is that part of us that knows that we have been mistreated. And if you want to cry, let it all out too; sadness and grief are very much an essential part of the process, just as anger is.

- **Learn to focus on the power of presence through mindfulness.** Being mindful means that you are attuned to yourself. You know yourself, what you need, and what you don't need. Slowing down and connecting to the deepest parts of ourselves puts us in a space where we can validate and acknowledge our pain and trauma. This is far better and more productive than using unhealthier coping mechanisms to try and forget about your pain.

- Also, because mindfulness helps us to connect to the power of now, our past and our trauma will start to have less of an impact on us. I always say that healing happens "in the right now," not in the past where our trauma lies. Sure, we are allowed to revisit trauma so that we can uncover the wounds and release the pain, but it isn't at all helpful to stay there for too long.

- **Practice patience with yourself.** If you're constantly scabbing and picking at a wound, you're doing more harm than good. If you exercise for days on end without rest, your muscles will be put under a lot of strain and that's going to start impacting your performance. The same logic applies to emotional healing as well. You should not place a deadline on our healing process. Rushing yourself will only place you under unnecessary stress— stress that you don't need. Instead, breathe, anchor yourself, and pat yourself on the back for the progress you're making.

- **Journal your way to healing.** I wrote my way into healing, believe it or not. I think that the pen and paper gave me the courage to explore the kinds of feelings and emotions that I was afraid to explore and to express by myself. Journaling is a proven coping mechanism for exploring complex emotions such as the grief of ending a relationship, or the process that comes from healing from a toxic relationship.

It's an opportunity to reflect on your behaviors, your mood, and any actions that you need to take. That process of putting things on paper is what allows you to gain clarity and a new perspective; something to help you slow down and relax.

The best part about journaling is that there are no rules or a set process. It's just you, the pen in your hand, and the freedom to express yourself as freely as you want to. When it's just you and that pen and paper, you don't have to pretend to be anyone else but yourself. You can be as raw and unfiltered as you want to be.

Here are some journal prompts that got me through those initial stages of healing:

1. What are the emotions that I'm currently feeling? What triggered them?

2. What are some healthy coping mechanisms that I can use when feeling overwhelmed?

3. What are some self-care activities that I can engage in to help me feel better?

4. What are some limiting beliefs that I have about myself that may be contributing to my emotional pain?

5. What are some positive affirmations that I can say to myself to counteract these limiting beliefs?

6. What do I need to forgive myself or others for?

7. What are some things that I'm grateful for in my life?

8. What are some things that I can let go of that are no longer serving me?

9. What are some things that I can do to cultivate more joy and happiness in my life?

10. What are some healthy boundaries that I can set with others to protect my emotional well-being?

11. What are some ways that I can practice mindfulness to be present in the moment?

12. What are some ways that I can practice vulnerability to connect with others on a deeper level?

My healing journey taught me a lot about what I'm willing and not willing to tolerate. It taught me that I should be unequivocally unapologetic about the kind of love that I know I deserve. What I found attractive changed tremendously when I made my way back to me again. Safety is so attractive. So are emotional maturity, accountability, consistency, and effort.

Know what's not attractive? Hot and cold behavior. When a person's words don't match their actions, the kind of people that I want and am attracted to right now are different from what a past version of me would have tolerated and accepted from a partner—I love that for me.

Chapter 5:

Understanding Your Triggers

Our triggers are messengers. When you can't trust the good moments of your life and allow yourself to feel good, to enjoy them without shame, to feel pleasure, or relax, then that is a sign that there is some part of us that still needs to heal. We may think that we're over something, but that one thing can put a cog in our wheel

Sometimes, our triggers are like a fire alarm, sounding off at the slightest hint of danger. They may be warning us of a situation that reminds us of past trauma or a vulnerability we feel.

Other times, they are like a pressure cooker, building up steam until they explode with a force that can be difficult to contain. These triggers often stem from a sense of injustice—a perceived violation of our values or boundaries.

And on some (well, most occasions), they can also guide us toward what is important to us. They may reveal our deepest desires, our core values, and our most cherished relationships.

Ultimately, our emotional triggers are a part of us—a unique blueprint that makes us who we are. By understanding and embracing our triggers, we can learn to navigate the complex landscape of our emotions and live a more fulfilling life.

Our emotional triggers differ and are incredibly diverse. What triggers me may not necessarily trigger you.

The Triggers

Now, we're going to work on unpacking the different kinds of triggers, what they mean, and how we can start dissolving them. Let's start with anger.

Anger

I like to think of our emotions as a set of buttons that can be pushed by different environmental stimuli. Anger is one of these buttons—like a fire alarm that goes off when there's danger or a threat to our well-being.

For example, imagine you're walking in a dark alley at night and someone suddenly jumps out and tries to attack you. Your body goes into fight-or-flight mode, and you might feel angry as you prepare to defend yourself. In this scenario, anger is like a trigger that prepares you for action, helping you to fight back or flee to safety.

Another analogy that we can use to think of anger is a boiling pot of water. When the heat is turned up, the water starts to bubble and eventually boils over. Similarly, when we experience a trigger that makes us angry, our emotions can start to boil over and spill out in the form of yelling, screaming, or even physical aggression.

And, in some instances, our anger can also be like a pressure valve that needs to be released. Imagine you're at work and your boss has been piling on the stress and pressure for weeks. You might feel increasingly frustrated and irritable until you finally reach a breaking point and explode in anger. In this scenario, anger is like a release valve that helps to relieve some of the built-up tension and stress.

By understanding how anger works and what triggers it, we can learn to manage it better. Most times, I have come to learn and understand that anger is usually a sign that we have somehow neglected ourselves somewhere because anger is a buildup of all the instances where we couldn't stand up and express ourselves.

The more we speak up, the more we realize how small we used to make ourselves in the presence of others or that narcissistic partner. We begin to see how we often exchanged our comfort for those people who didn't have our best interests at heart; that's why we all so suddenly become flooded with that tsunami of anger toward the people we love and, sometimes, the strangers in our lives.

Resentment

Resentment tells us that our boundaries have been crossed or that we have abandoned ourselves. I like to think of resentment as a venomous serpent that's coiled tightly around our hearts—it stands ready to strike at any moment. It simmers beneath the surface, a fit of seething anger boiling just below the skin, waiting for an opportunity to lash out.

Imagine this: Let's hypothetically say that you and your partner work together. You're at work, and they take credit for a project you worked tirelessly on. You'll feel your blood boiling as your resentment toward them builds. You won't be able to shake the feeling that you've been wronged, and each time you see or interact with them, your anger intensifies.

Or, perhaps in that same romantic relationship, your partner continuously disregards your feelings and needs. You feel invisible, insignificant, and unimportant. What will happen is that those feelings of bitterness and hurt are going to build up and begin to fester into resentment.

Resentment can be triggered by a multitude of situations, from minor grievances to major betrayals. It's an emotion that grows slowly over time and is often fueled by a sense of injustice or unfairness. And when it reaches its boiling point, it explodes into a fiery rage, leaving a trail of destruction in its wake.

So, be aware of the signs of clenched fists, gritted teeth, and seething anger. Because once the serpent of resentment takes hold, it's hard to break free from its grip.

You can't support or love other people if it means that you have to betray yourself and your unique needs constantly. When you are unhappy, you will start to look to blame others. You believe you are unhappy because others are asking too much of you. When you take accountability for setting healthy boundaries in your own life, you will no longer feel the need to resent people, because when you set and enforce boundaries, you take your power back.

Loneliness

Loneliness is the experience of not feeling seen.

Imagine yourself stranded on a deserted island with nobody else but you. You feel alone and disconnected from the world. This sense of sadness and despair creeps up on you and that grows stronger with each passing moment. It's as if a trigger has been pulled inside you, setting off a chain reaction of negative emotions.

This is what loneliness feels like—a cascade of negative feelings, such as sadness and despair, and even physical pain. It's like a switch has been flipped inside you, and it's telling you that something is missing in your life. Just as with hunger or thirst, loneliness is a signal that your body and mind need something that you're not sufficiently providing.

We need to understand that loneliness isn't just something we experience when we're alone. It's something we can even experience in crowded rooms with no one to interact with. It's caused by surrounding ourselves with people who neither see nor understand us. It tells us that we need to connect with others and build meaningful relationships.

Just as food and water are essential for our survival, social connection is essential for our well-being. Being seen, heard, and understood is something that is at the core of deep connection. These are the types of connections that make us feel less alone in the world; the types of connections that make us feel as if we matter in the world and this life.

When you're feeling lonely, it's important to reach out to others, whether it's through a phone call, a text message, or a face-to-face conversation. By doing so, you can start to build the connections that you need to feel fulfilled and happy. That one moment of genuine contact with someone will do more to help you feel connected than a full day of surface-level interactions with someone.

Relationships are about quality and not quantity. Also, the relationships that we have with ourselves go a long way in getting rid of loneliness. Get to know who you are, what you like, and what you want. And lastly, one meaningful relationship will do so much to pull you out of that experience of being alone.

Guilt

Guilt is like that tiny pebble that gets stuck in your shoe while hiking. At first, it starts as just a minor annoyance, but as you continue down the trail, the pebble starts to rub against your foot and cause you great discomfort. It works the same way; when we feel guilty in a relationship, it's like there's this small issue that's bothering us, but we don't address it right away. Over time, that feeling of guilt grows and becomes an even bigger problem that affects the overall health of the relationship.

Guilt is that place that tells us that we're living within the expectations of others and not our own; it's a sign that we've done or are doing something that goes against our values or the expectations of the relationship. For example, if you've promised to start speaking up when your partner crosses a boundary, but you end up giving in when push comes to shove, you might feel guilty because you know you've let yourself down. That feeling of guilt is trying to tell you that you need to make things right and start honoring yourself in the right way.

Guilt can also be a trigger for communication in a relationship. When we feel guilty, we might be more willing to open up and share our thoughts and feelings with the people around us. For example, if you feel guilty about something, your partner said during an argument, you might be more likely to approach them to try to work through the issue.

Guilt can be a useful tool in relationships if only we listen to what it is trying to tell us and use it as an opportunity to honor ourselves. But, if we ignore our feelings of guilt or let them fester, they can become a bigger problem that damages our state of emotional and mental well-being.

Bitterness

Our bitterness is trying to tell us that there is resentment that we've been holding on to for far too long. Think of it as a sharp and acrid flavor that leaves a lingering aftertaste in your mouth after biting into something undesirable. In toxic relationships, bitterness is a trigger that leaves a lasting emotional impact. It stems from feelings of resentment, disappointment, and anger that have built up over time.

Imagine you have been with someone for several years. You have had your fair share of ups and downs, but lately, you have been arguing more frequently and becoming increasingly unhappy with the relationship. At some point or another, you're going to start to feel bitter toward your partner, holding onto past grievances and resentments, which can lead to a toxic dynamic in the relationship.

Bitterness wants to tell us that something is wrong in the relationship and needs to be addressed. It may be a sign that one or both people in the relationship are not communicating effectively or that there are unresolved issues that need to be worked through. It can also indicate a lack of trust or respect in the relationship.

Left unchecked, bitterness poisons our relationships. It is a reminder to us that relationships take effort and require ongoing communication and work to stay healthy and strong. By recognizing and addressing feelings of bitterness, we can take steps toward building a healthier and happier relationship with our partners.

Judgment

Judgment can be likened to a loaded gun. It is a trigger that sets off a chain reaction of devaluation, projection, and gaslighting. Essentially, it tells the narcissist that their fragile ego and sense of self-worth are threatened.

Imagine a scenario where your narcissistic partner comes home late after a night out with their friends. You express concern and disappointment about the lateness. This triggers them to feel judged and criticized, leading to them lashing out and accusing you of being controlling, suffocating, and untrusting. Then, you are left confused and guilty, wondering what you did wrong.

Judgment is trying to tell us that our narcissistic partners have incredibly fragile egos that are easily wounded. They can't tolerate any form of criticism, feedback, or correction. It feels like a direct attack on their sense of self to them. They will often react aggressively or defensively, projecting their insecurities onto others.

It is important to recognize and understand this trigger in narcissistic relationships. By doing so, we can learn to navigate interactions with narcissists in a way that is less harmful to ourselves and others.

Dealing With Your Triggers

I like to think of our emotions as I think of the ocean. Sometimes, they are calm and soothing, and on other occasions, they are a stormy and dangerous whirlwind. Just as sailors need to be prepared for the sometimes unexpected storms, we also need to learn how to deal with our emotional triggers.

These triggers are often like hidden rocks beneath the surface, waiting to wreck our ship of calmness and peace. They can be anything from a word, gesture, or memory that ignites a powerful emotional reaction within us, such as anger, fear, or sadness.

It's easy to feel overwhelmed by these emotions, like being caught in a fierce current that drags us away from our safe harbor. But as skilled sailors know how to navigate through storms, we too can learn how to manage our emotional triggers and stay afloat. With the right tools and strategies, we can steer our ship toward a brighter horizon, where the waters are calm and our emotions are under control. So, let's hoist the sails and embark on a journey of self-discovery and emotional mastery!

Become more emotionally aware. Keep a journal that will help you identify and note down the instances and situations where you feel triggered. For instance, is it when your partner criticizes you for something such as your appearance, or when they shift the blame and try to make you feel guilty about something that you shouldn't even have to feel guilty about? Make a note of all these instances so that you can be on your way toward your healing journey.

Work on rewiring your negative thinking. You see, the thing about our triggers is that they are exceptional at making us believe all sorts of negative things about ourselves. But, a lot of the things they try to convince us of are absolute lies. These are some of the things that I said to myself (Note: I still remind myself of these because they are applicable in whatever season):

- "I'm worthy of love and respect, regardless of what my ex-partner may have said or done."

- "I have the power to break free from the cycle of abuse and create a happy, healthy future for myself."

- "My worth is not determined by the opinions of others, especially those who seek to diminish me."

- "I'm capable of healing from this trauma and emerging stronger and more resilient than ever before."

- "I refuse to let my ex-partner's toxic behavior define me or limit my potential."

- "I deserve to surround myself with people who uplift and support me, not tear me down."

- "I'm not responsible for my ex-partner's actions or emotions, and I refuse to take on that burden."

- "I choose to focus on my growth and well-being rather than dwelling on the past or seeking revenge."

- "I'm worthy of forgiveness and compassion, both from myself and others."

- "I'm capable of setting healthy boundaries and advocating for myself, even in the face of resistance or manipulation."

Practice saying and doing the things that you were once too afraid to say while in a relationship with that narcissistic partner. To get comfortable with the uncomfortable, we have to familiarize ourselves with the uncomfortable. In those moments where you are just tempted to simply agree with someone without voicing your opinion, use this sentence as a framework to help guide you: "I disagree because…" Sometimes, certain behaviors need to be practiced for them to sink in and become even more real.

Show up for yourself from a place of curiosity, rather than judgment; instead of asking yourself why it's taking such a long time for you to heal, or why you can't just "get over it. Recognize and embrace the fact that you are human and that sometimes we go through difficult things. Being open-minded in this sense will make the process a lot easier for you to navigate and help you grow and foster patience toward yourself.

It's incredibly liberating and empowering to know and understand that you have all the power that you need to meet your own needs. And during those times when you feel that you are incapable of fully meeting your own needs, try to see if there are small things that you can do to try and address what is missing. Next time, when you feel triggered, simply ask yourself, *What is it that I need most right now, and what can I give to myself at this moment to fill this gap?* The answers can be:

- *Right now, I need validation. I knew that I showed up as best as I could, so I must not push or punish myself by thinking that I didn't do enough.*

- *Right now, I need to be understood, so I'm going to process this with someone who I trust.*

Lastly, I want to tell you that I see you, I hear you, and I'm rooting for you along the way.

Chapter 6:

Trusting Yourself Again

Are you looking for answers outside of yourself? A close friend recently said something to me that struck me deeply. She told me that at times, it seemed to her that I was outsourcing my power. And you know what, as hard as it was to admit, I knew at that moment when she said those words to me that she was right. For the longest time, I was that person who wanted to get all the answers from someone else.

I wanted them to tell me what it is specifically that I should do because I thought that other people knew better than me. I wanted them to give me the key that would unlock all of the doubt that I carried within me and lead me to a place of certainty. Part of this also meant that I didn't believe that I held the key to fully trusting myself.

But you know what I have come to learn: Our bodies carry a deep and infinite wisdom within them. We have more answers than we think we do. Sometimes, I guess that we need a person to nudge us toward that place gently; to gently guide us home and help us find our inner wisdom so that we can remember how wise and intelligent we truly are.

Self-trust is something that I see a lot of people struggling with on their journey, but remember that without self-trust, we can't get to the place where we truly want to be. If you can't trust yourself, then you can't possibly expect others to trust you too. You are the one who is in control. Let's start by taking a look at what self-trust looks like:

- It looks like paying close attention to your needs and honoring them.

- It's creating space for your thoughts.

- It's building healthier habits for yourself and developing healthier coping mechanisms.

- It's laying the foundation of your own values.

- It's teaching and encouraging yourself to become comfortable with vulnerability.

- Most importantly, it's keeping your promises to yourself.

Self-trust sounds pretty cool and all, but you know the one thing about it is that it is not always the easiest of things to do. It is like a tender flower that needs to be nurtured and cared for to bloom. However, sometimes, life's many challenges can make it feel like that flower is being trampled on, leaving us feeling unsure and unsteady. It's like trying to walk on a tightrope without a safety net—the fear of falling can be paralyzing.

Imagine you're standing at the edge of a cliff, looking out at the vast expanse of the ocean below. You know that you can jump off and swim to safety, but the fear of the unknown keeps you frozen in place. The same can be said for self-trust—we know that we can make decisions and trust ourselves, but instead, that doubt creeps in. We take a step back and leave without having taken our big leap.

Reclaiming You: Steps to Learning to Trust Yourself Again

You are the best project that you will ever work on. Focusing on trusting yourself is something that won't ever end wrongly because choosing to reclaim the identity that was silenced by others for so long is truly the most loving thing that you can do for yourself. Below are the steps that you can take to start trusting your brilliant and beautiful self again after years of losing your voice.

Acknowledge Your Experience

Acknowledge and do not deny yourself the validity of your experience. The first step toward building self-trust is to acknowledge the experiences that have led you to doubt yourself. Recognize that you have been in a toxic relationship and that this experience has likely left you feeling confused, hurt, and uncertain about your abilities and judgments.

Set Small Goals

Building self-trust is a process that takes time, so it's important to set small, achievable goals along the way. Start by identifying one area of your life where you would like to build more confidence and set a goal that is specific, measurable, and realistic. Let's say your goal is to increase interaction with others and build your social circle. After leaving my abusive relationship, I found that I struggled to engage with people. I was shy and afraid to venture out, yet I was lonely and craved connection.

As running is one of my hobbies, I joined an online group for runners in my community. I developed some great connections with people online and worked my way up to eventually joining a group of them for a Saturday morning run. A couple of these group members are some of my closest friends today!

Local Facebook groups are an excellent way to virtually meet people in your area who share similar interests. This is a great starting point if you are apprehensive about physically meeting people, and can help you gradually move to having in-person connections.

If, on the other hand, you enjoy face-to-face interaction right off the hop, commit to taking leisurely walks and saying hello to at least one person along the way. Grabbing a coffee at your favorite coffee shop? Pay a genuine compliment to a stranger. Who knows where these small interactions might take you? They may develop into meaningful conversations that lead to budding friendships!

Hold Yourself Accountable

Be willing to hold yourself accountable. Self-accountability matters when you're on your journey of building self-trust. Just as a skilled tightrope walker relies on their balance and focuses to make it across a high wire, we too must rely on our commitment to personal growth to build that strong foundation of self-trust.

Imagine yourself as the tightrope walker. You're poised at the starting point of a long, narrow wire suspended high above the ground. As you begin making your way across the wire, you must maintain your focus, be balanced, and be accountable for every step you take. You can't blame the wind, the height, or any other external factor for your success or failure. The only thing that matters is your ability to stay focused and accountable for every step you take.

It works the same way when building self-trust, we must take responsibility for our actions, thoughts, and emotions. We can't blame others for our lack of progress or success. Instead, we must hold ourselves accountable, acknowledging our mistakes along the way and taking steps to correct them. By doing so, we demonstrate to ourselves that we are capable of taking control of our lives and making positive changes.

Just like the tightrope walker must trust in their abilities to make it across the wire, we too must trust in ourselves to navigate the ups and downs of life with integrity, resilience, and accountability. In doing so, we can build that strong unshakeable foundation that will serve us well in all areas of our lives.

Celebrate Your Victories

Celebrate your victories, however big or small they might be. When you achieve your goals, take time to celebrate your successes. This can help reinforce your confidence and build momentum toward your next goal.

Set Internal Boundaries

Self-trust has also taught me a lot about setting internal boundaries. It's not just about what you say to other people, but what you say to yourself as well and how you stick with that. And it doesn't have to be big elaborate things. It can be simple things like being more intentional about who you choose to follow on social media or making sure that you do the things that you say you're going to do.

The trust we build within ourselves will take us pretty far. Here are some simple ways that you can also start setting and enforcing better boundaries with yourself:

- following through on your word and the things that you say you're going to do

- sticking to your values and beliefs

- defining your limits and upholding them

- avoiding interactions with people who drain you or make you feel bad about yourself

- saying no when you want to say no and saying yes when you want to say yes

I have my own back. The question is, do you have yours? And oh, too often we confuse that with the "big things," but really, it's all about those tiny moments in your day where you make the conscious choice to not sell yourself short, or inflict any unnecessary pain and suffering toward yourself for simply being a human being.

To close this chapter, here are a final few reminders on self-trust for you to keep holding on to:

- If the promises that you make to yourself are manageable enough, you will be able to uphold them on your hardest days. That's when you also know that you'll be able to build self-trust forevermore. These promises don't have to be grand or elaborate, they can be as simple as promising to eat breakfast tomorrow morning or promising to wash your hair. These might seem insignificant, but the more you follow through and celebrate these as the wins they are, the more you begin to increase your trust in, and respect for, yourself.

- All that self-trust asks of us is to be with our innate truth, rather than berating ourselves for not being better.

- There is no right and wrong way to "trust yourself," your inner wisdom will guide you to exactly where you need to be. Just focus on doing one small thing and on showing up as imperfectly as you can.

Self-trust is going to involve a willingness to take risks, embracing vulnerability, and knowing that rejection or fear is not a reflection of your worth or capabilities.

Chapter 7:

Trusting Others Again

Trust is a fragile thing. It takes time to build and can be shattered in an instant. When you've been in a toxic relationship, your trust may have been broken so many times that it feels impossible to ever trust again. But as you begin to heal, you may start to realize that trust is a necessary component of any healthy relationship. Learning to trust again can be a daunting task, but it's not impossible.

At first, trust may seem like a foreign concept to you. You may feel like you're walking on eggshells, constantly second-guessing everything that others say and do. It's natural to feel this way, given what you've been through. However, it's important to remember that not everyone is like your ex. Not everyone will hurt you or take advantage of you.

Think of trust as a beautiful crystal vase. It's delicate and valuable, and it takes time and care to create. When you enter into a new relationship, you place your trust in that person as you would place the vase in their hands. You hope that they will handle it with care and keep it safe. When you've been in a toxic relationship, it's like the vase has been dropped and shattered into a million pieces.

Your trust has been broken so many times that it feels like it can never be repaired. You're left with a pile of broken shards, and you're afraid to pick them up for fear of getting hurt again.

Now, imagine that someone comes along and offers to help you put the vase back together. At first, you may be hesitant to accept their help. You may be afraid that they will drop the vase again or that it will never be the same as it was before. It's natural to feel this way, given what you've been through.

But if you're willing to take a chance and work on putting the vase back together, you may find that it's stronger and more beautiful than ever before. It may take time and effort, and there may be some bumps along the way, but with patience and care, you can rebuild your trust and create something extraordinary.

What I've Learned

My journey of learning to trust others has been a challenging and incredibly rewarding one. There are many beautiful lessons that I've learned along the way and here's what they are.

It Starts With Us

If you can first learn to trust yourself, you are on the right path. My trust radar is pretty strong, so I've learned that when my gut intuition tells me something, it's usually pretty right. If you can first learn to trust yourself, you are on the right path—much like a proficient mariner who knows how to navigate like the back of their hand. You can chart a course for your life that is unfailingly true to your inner compass.

And just as a seasoned sailor trusts the signals of the sea, your trust radar can guide you toward the people, places, and opportunities that align with your values and deepest desires. So, when your gut intuition speaks, listen closely because it's likely leading you toward a fulfilling and purposeful path.

Trust Is Earned

Not everyone has earned the right to hear your story. As you navigate your journey, you are going to learn and become more discerning about who truly deserves to hear your story.

Your journey is personal and intimate, and the insights and lessons you've learned along the way have shaped you into the person you are today. You deserve to be discerning and selective about who you invite into your life to hear your story.

It's important to recognize that not everyone is equipped to handle the depth and complexity of your experiences. Some may not have the empathy or understanding to truly appreciate what you've been through, while others may have hidden agendas for seeking out your story.

By being selective about who you share your story with, you're not only protecting yourself but also honoring the power and value of your journey. Don't hesitate to take your time and be cautious in deciding who deserves to hear your story—you'll know when you've found the right person who can truly appreciate and learn from your experience.

It's Difficult and That's Okay

Trust is a vulnerable thing. When we open ourselves up to trusting someone, we relinquish a certain amount of our emotions to them. When we open ourselves up to trust, we're essentially handing over a piece of our hearts to someone else. It's not an easy thing to do and can leave you feeling incredibly vulnerable and scared. But when we find someone worthy of that trust, it's also one of the most beautiful feelings in the world.

In a way, it's like a delicate dance. We take hesitant steps toward someone, slowly opening up more and more as they prove themselves worthy of our trust. Eventually, we're able to let our guard down completely and truly connect with that person on a deep level.

But just as easily as trust is given, it can also be taken away. The slightest misstep can shatter that fragile bundle of emotions, leaving us feeling exposed. It feels amazing being your full, authentic, and realistic self, so chiseling at that wall that you've built around you is going to take a whole lot of time. So, it's okay if you choose to take it piece by piece, moment by moment.

Learning to Trust Again

Learning to trust again is a process. It won't happen overnight, and there may be setbacks along the way. But with time, patience, and a willingness to open yourself up to new experiences, you can learn to trust again and build healthy, fulfilling relationships. Here are a few takeaway tips that you can keep with you as you work on navigating this journey of learning to trust others again.

- **Believe people that very first time when they show you who they are.** Sometimes, when we meet people or are falling in love, there's that little part of our brains that tells us, "Hey, maybe I can actually change them just a little bit," but the truth is that trying to change someone who refuses to take responsibility for their actions is like trying to teach a goldfish to play fetch. No matter how much you toss that tennis ball, the goldfish will never bring it back.

  Similarly, no amount of reasoning or pleading will make someone confront their mistakes if they're not willing to acknowledge their role in them. It's like trying to hammer a nail into a marshmallow—there's no solid ground to work with. So, instead of wasting your time and energy on an impossible task, it's better to focus on your growth and surround yourself with people who share your values of accountability and personal responsibility.

- **Learn to put yourself first.** I want you to read that line again. You come first. Not them. You do not have to minimize or make yourself feel uncomfortable just to accommodate the needs of others. You don't have to people-please your way through life to get people to like you. Remind yourself over and over again:

  o "It's not my job to keep the peace or to keep them happy."

  o "My needs are just as important as their needs."

- "My opinions matter too."

- "I'm not responsible for the behaviors of those around me."

- "I don't have to be available all the time."

Remember, it's not about being selfish, it's simply just about being smart. When you know how remarkable you are and what your worth is, others will begin to see it as well and treat you in the way that you deserve to be treated. If they don't, you know you have the choice to cut them off because it simply means they are not your people.

- **Rediscover who you are.** Connect with the you that you were before the narcissist got a hold of you. Uncover your strengths again. Remind yourself of the majestic power you hold, the courage you have, and most importantly, the beauty in you that survives all that you did. You are still you. And you are still there; all that is needed is a little bit of courage to unmask and peek right through the veil that is covering the very essence of who you are.

- **Look for the green flags as well.** I think that oftentimes in relationships, we get so caught up and focus too much on the things that we should watch out for, which is understandable because we do want to guard our hearts and don't want to be reckless with who we let back into our lives. But you wanna know what else is pretty cool? Focusing on all the things that they are doing right as well. This can look like:

  - people who encourage you to have and build a life of your own, and not just a life that revolves around them

  - when they apologize and take accountability for their actions

  - when they are comfortable with expressing their vulnerabilities and the things that scare them

- o when they make you feel seen, heard, understood, and acknowledged

- o when they support you when you're are struggling and don't just become dismissive of your emotions

- o when their actions align with the words coming out of their mouths

- **Take things slowly.** Don't rush into new relationships or friendships. Take the time to get to know people and build a foundation of trust. This may mean setting boundaries and communicating your needs and expectations clearly.

And oh, don't forget the never-ending process of doing healing work. This involves therapy, self-care, and learning to love yourself again. You see, healing emotional wounds is a lot like fixing a leaky faucet in your heart—it takes time and effort, but once it's done, the water flows smoothly, and you can finally stop using that bucket to catch your tears. When we take the time to address our emotional baggage, we can start to recognize our worth and set healthy boundaries in our relationships.

It can also be likened to building a sturdy fence around a garden—we can let people in, but we also know when to say no to the weeds that threaten to take over. By giving ourselves the space we need to grow and thrive, we become more capable of nurturing healthy relationships without sacrificing our well-being. It's like having a perfectly balanced see-saw—we can enjoy the ride without getting stuck at either end. Essentially, I'm saying that when you feel more confident and comfortable in your own skin, you'll be better equipped to trust others.

Friend, when we get to a place where we can assert our worth; when we get to that place where we know who we are and are unafraid of setting boundaries that we need; and when we refuse to allow people to make us feel powerless in our own skin, we can then let go of the fear of being hurt again. There will be people in this world who we can't trust—that's something that we sadly can't change, but we can't allow that to prevent us from coming in-between the people who deserve to get the very best of who we are.

Keep going. I know you can do it!

Chapter 8:

Building Your Community

Climbing a mountain can be an incredibly challenging but rewarding experience. Whether you're a seasoned or novice mountaineer, you'll quickly realize that it's not the kind of journey that you can embark on alone. It's easy to get lost, stumble over rocks, or lose your footing on steep inclines. However, with a team of supportive climbers or friends and family by your side, you can overcome these challenges and make it safely to the top.

In many ways, life is also like climbing a mountain. It's full of twists and turns, ups and downs, and unexpected obstacles. Whether you're navigating a challenging career, personal situation, or relationship dynamics, you'll quickly realize that you can't do it alone.

Having a community who share your values and vision can make all the difference. They can help you navigate tough decisions, provide support when you stumble, and give you the motivation to keep going when the climb gets tough. It's such a beautiful thing.

You'll find that the healing journey is similar. It takes a village to mend a broken heart, shattered spirit, or wounded body. As much as we'd like to believe that we're strong enough to do it all on our own, we aren't. No man is an island. However, reaching out for help can be one of the scariest things to do. It requires vulnerability, trust, and that deep understanding that we need that sense of togetherness.

I want to tell you that there is hope. There are people out there willing to walk with us through our pain, struggles, and fears. People who will hold our hand and lend us their strength when ours is running low. People who will listen without judgment, love without conditions, and offer us the kind of compassion that can only come from those who have walked a similar path.

The road to healing is never easy, but it is always worth it. And when we allow ourselves to be held and uplifted by a loving and supportive community, we can find the courage to take those first steps toward wholeness. So, let us reach out to those around us, let us be vulnerable and ask for help when we need it, and let us trust that there are people out there who are willing to walk through it all with us. Together, we can find the healing we so desperately seek.

Community Building Tips

There's a lot that I learned about healing and sisterhood throughout my journey! I learned that instead of doing life alone, I would much rather go about doing life with people who I know I can count on. Before we get to the tips on building a community, here are some things that I have learned about community and sisterhood.

It's an incredible blessing and a great privilege to have a confidante that you can talk to about stuff that isn't so easy. The greatest and most supportive people are the ones that will literally stop you from stepping into a raging fire, but rather into your greatness.

It encourages self-care! Being a part of a supportive community truly does help us to prioritize self-care and the things that nourish the mind, body, and soul.

It's incredibly empowering. I have learned that before we can fully honor and love and appreciate others for who and what they are, we must first know and understand how we can love and honor ourselves first. When we ourselves are empowered and unafraid to walk in our radiance, we open up the gateway for the other women around us to do the same.

In safe spaces (in community and sisterhood), you don't have to be afraid to show off the very best of who you are. You come as you are, and you will be accepted as such and not pushed away.

My wish for you right now is that you would always remember that there are people out there with good souls; people who have your best interests at heart. I know that it sometimes feels hard to believe that this can at all in any way or form be true, but it is. Not everyone out there is going to hurt you. So, don't close that beautiful heart of yours off to the world and miss out on a wonderful opportunity and experience. You'll miss out on being loved unconditionally.

I love to believe that there are people out there who are for me; people who understand me and are willing to welcome me in all my brokenness. So, I'll work hard at finding and nurturing my relationships with those people. Here are six tips for you to keep in mind as you build and solidify your community of people:

- **Find a support group.** No one understands us better than the people who have gone through similar experiences as us. Seek out a group of people who have gone through similar experiences. Sharing your story with others who understand what you're going through can help you feel less isolated and give you a sense of belonging.

- **Reach out to friends and family.** I think that we sometimes distance ourselves from our friends and our family because we are afraid of being a burden, but that's hardly the case. The people who love us want to see us in a happy, healthy, and striving state. Don't be afraid to lean on those closest to you. Let them know how they can support you as you heal.

- **Consider therapy.** The thought of opening up to a stranger doesn't sound all that palatable. I completely understand, but professional help can provide valuable guidance and support during the healing process. Also, the benefit of talking to a therapist is that you don't have to hold back on anything, whereas when you are talking with a family member or a friend, you might be tempted to hold back or leave out certain details of your experience. Therapy is one of the safest spaces you can find.

- **Join a Facebook group.** This is for people who have gone through a similar experience as you. You can also use an online therapy service like BetterHelp. The truth is that therapy can be expensive, and it's not something that everyone can afford. Still, with modern technology and the accessibility of the internet, we do have the option of connecting with people online who can help us walk through the journey and offer a bit of wise advice to help us on our healing journeys.

- **Immerse yourself in activities you enjoy.** Before healing, I had somewhat forgotten how much joy writing used to bring me. In healing, I picked up my pen and was reminded of how much strength it used to give me. So, I wrote, and wrote, and wrote, and never stopped. Look at me now, I have written a whole book! If writing isn't your cup of tea, you can maybe join a club, take a class, or find a hobby that makes you feel incredibly alive. Connecting with others while doing something you love can give you a sense of purpose and fulfillment.

- **Volunteer.** You can never go wrong with acts of kindness. Giving back to others is a great way to build connections and find a sense of purpose. Find a cause you're passionate about and volunteer your time to help others.

If you battle to put one foot in front of the other, it's okay if you get up on your knees and crawl. That is far much better than staying stuck in the same place for an eternity. Take it one day at a time and be patient with yourself. You deserve to heal and find happiness again.

Conclusion

Healing is a lot like learning to ride a wave—it's a wild, unpredictable journey that can take you to unexpected places. Sometimes, you'll feel like you're on top of the world, effortlessly gliding over the water with the wind in your hair and the sun on your skin. Other times, you'll be knocked down by a powerful force and struggle to find your footing again. But just like a skilled surfer, those who have mastered the art of healing know how to navigate the ups and downs of life with grace and resilience.

They understand that every wave is an opportunity to learn, grow, and become stronger and that the key to success is to keep riding, no matter how rough the waters may get. The one thing that I want you to take from this is that you are going to make your way back to shore—to the dry and firm land. All you need is the courage to take that first leap of faith and ride the wave toward a brighter tomorrow—and a better you!

So darling, in case you don't believe it, or haven't told yourself as of late: You are going to be okay. And you know why I know that is? Because you're waking up every day and choosing to do life. You get up and out of bed, brush your teeth, wash your face, and do something small for yourself. I know that on some days or some moments, it feels downright nearly impossible, but you are trying, and that is what makes you so damn powerful!

You know, sometimes, we have these things in life happen to us that make us feel ungrounded; things that cause us to lose ourselves. It's normal and that's what other people's behaviors tend to do to us. But, remember that even though we don't have the power to change what life throws at us, we can certainly do the following:

- choose how we're going to respond and act toward the situation

- set boundaries and protect our sense of peace

- choose to shift perspective and rather focus on the things that do matter to us

- express gratitude for the mere fact that we are still here and thriving through life

- choose to focus on the lessons that we pick up along the way

- get to choose to focus on the present moment

- reframe our negative thinking and challenge that urge to overthink

- choose to come back home to the people who we truly want to be

Now, go out there, live your life, and continue to create enough space for all the beautiful things that the world has to offer. I'm rooting for you!

Next Steps

Thank you for allowing me to share my story with you. I hope I left you with something that will stick with you as you navigate the days ahead. I would love it if you would leave a review on Amazon or wherever you purchased this book, as reviews help others who might benefit from this content, find this book.

References

Arzt, N. (n.d.). *How to set boundaries with a "narcissist"*. Talkspace Mental Health Conditions. https://www.talkspace.com/mental-health/conditions/articles/how-to-set-boundaries-with-a-narcissist/

Buck, C. (2017, November 21). *4 ways you can replace self-blame with self-care*. Hey Sigmund. https://www.heysigmund.com/self-blame-self-care/

Callahan & Blaine. (2021, August 25). *Sexual abuse in relationships*. https://www.callahan-law.com/sexual-abuse-in-relationships/

Corie Chu Healing. (2023, March 27). *Self-blame: When we do it & why do we do it?* https://coriechu.com/blog/self-blame-when-we-do-it-and-why-do-we-do-it

Davies, J. (2022, April 16). *12 reasons why narcissists and empaths are attracted to each other*. Learning Mind. https://www.learning-mind.com/narcissists-and-empaths-attraction/

Denning, T. (2019, December 9). *12 signs you'll be okay when life gets unexpectedly tough*. Medium. https://psiloveyou.xyz/12-signs-youll-be-okay-when-life-gets-unexpectedly-tough-ad98d94c83c0

Deschene, L. (2012, November 14). *5 ways to validate yourself: Be part of your support system*. Tiny Buddha. https://tinybuddha.com/blog/5-ways-to-validate-be-part-of-your-support-system/

Experience Life. (n.d.). *13 strategies to deal with your emotional triggers*. https://experiencelife.lifetime.life/article/13-strategies-to-deal-with-your-emotional-triggers/

Firestone, L. (2013, April 29). *In a relationship with a narcissist? A guide to narcissistic relationships.* PsychAlive. https://www.psychalive.org/narcissistic-relationships/

Fontaine, Z. (2021, August 1). *5 tips to relearn to trust after a toxic relationship.* Medium. https://zitafontaine.medium.com/5-tips-to-relearn-to-trust-after-a-toxic-relationship-7a69415681c9

Gelman & Associates. (2016, July 29). *Why is leaving a narcissist so hard?* https://lisagelman.com/divorce/leaving-narcissist-hard/

Glass, D. J. (2022, June 22). *Part I: What is gaslighting? 6 types of gaslighting techniques.* DivorceMag.com. https://www.divorcemag.com/blog/what-is-gaslighting-6-types-of-gaslighting

Good Therapy. (2013, June 11). *The psychology of triggers and how they affect mental health.* https://www.goodtherapy.org/blog/psychpedia/trigger

Gordon, S. (2019). *How to identify and cope with emotional abuse.* Verywell Mind. https://www.verywellmind.com/identify-and-cope-with-emotional-abuse-4156673

Gratitude Blog. (2021, June 16). *10 steps to love yourself again after a toxic relationship.* https://blog.gratefulness.me/how-to-love-yourself/

The Guest House. (2022, July 10). *What are "triggers" and how do they affect us?* https://www.theguesthouseocala.com/what-are-triggers-and-how-do-they-affect-us/

Hammond, C. (2015a, May 27). *How narcissists use money to abuse.* PsychCentral. https://psychcentral.com/pro/exhausted-woman/2015/05/how-narcissists-use-money-to-abuse

Hammond, C. (2015b, June 4). *The stages of narcissistic sexual abuse.* Psych Central. https://psychcentral.com/pro/exhausted-woman/2015/06/the-stages-of-narcissistic-sexual-abuse#1

Hip and Healthy. (2019, June 27). *10 traits of an empath.* https://hipandhealthy.com/10-traits-of-an-empath/

Holland, K. (2018, February 13). *How to recognize the signs of emotional manipulation and what to do.* Healthline. https://www.healthline.com/health/mental-health/emotional-manipulation

Ineffable Living. (2023, May 10). *Empaths and narcissists: Top 5 reasons why narcissists target empaths & how to starve the narcissist of supply.* https://ineffableliving.com/traits-that-make-empaths-perfect-targets-for-a-narcissist/

Kentucky Counseling Center. (2021, October 1). *How to deal with emotional triggers.* https://kentuckycounselingcenter.com/how-to-deal-with-emotional-triggers/

Krstic, Z., & Dolgoff, S. (2022, November 9). *50 best self-care ideas for mental and physical wellbeing.* Good Housekeeping. https://www.goodhousekeeping.com/health/wellness/g25643 343/self-care-ideas/

Lancer, D. (2019, December 22). *It's hard to leave a narcissist or abuser: Learn why and how.* Medium. https://medium.com/narcissism-and-abusive-relationships/it-hard-to-leave-a-narcissist-or-abuser-learn-why-and-how-a52914427ff9

Laub, E. (2022, August 29). *The 7 stages of trauma bonding.* Choosing Therapy. https://www.choosingtherapy.com/stages-of-trauma-bonding/

Martin, S. (2019, December 20). *17 ways to validate yourself.* Live Well With Sharon Martin. https://www.livewellwithsharonmartin.com/validate-yourself/

Neuharth, D. (2020, June 20). *7 ways to set boundaries with narcissists.* Psychology Today. https://www.psychologytoday.com/za/blog/narcissism-demystified/202006/7-ways-set-boundaries-narcissists

Pedersen, T. (2022, April 28). *Triggers: What they are, how they form, and what to do.* PsychCentral. https://psychcentral.com/lib/what-is-a-trigger

Pommerenk, D. A. (2022, March 17). *Why you keep begging your narcissist to try again and how to stop.* Medium. https://apommerenk.medium.com/why-you-keep-begging-your-narcissist-to-try-again-and-how-to-stop-1695f2064ddc

Raypole, C. (2019, November 25). *What is an empath? 15 signs and traits.* Healthline. https://www.healthline.com/health/what-is-an-empath

Robinson, M. (2018, June 6). *How to get and keep your healing.* Kenneth Copeland Ministries. https://blog.kcm.org/receive-keep-healing/

Salters-Pedneault, K. (2022). *What you can do to help others feel validated.* Verywell Mind. https://www.verywellmind.com/what-is-emotional-validation-425336

Sharewell. (2023, March 1). *Leaving a toxic relationship: How to build a strong support system.* https://blog.sharewellnow.com/inspiration/leaving-a-toxic-relationship-how-to-building-a-strong-support-system/

Steber, C. (2019, March 2). *7 reasons why it's so difficult to leave an unhealthy relationship.* Bustle. https://www.bustle.com/p/7-reasons-why-its-so-difficult-to-leave-unhealthy-relationship-16003317

Stern, R. (2018, December 19). *Gaslighting in relationships: How to spot it and shut it down.* Vox. https://www.vox.com/first-person/2018/12/19/18140830/gaslighting-relationships-politics-explained

Stieg, C. (2017, December 4). *11 tips for learning to trust in a new relationship.* Refinery29. https://www.refinery29.com/en-us/trust-issues-new-relationship

Sytsma, J. (2020, February 28). *How to trust in a new relationship after being betrayed.* Relationship Reality 312. https://www.relationshipreality312.com/how-to-trust-in-a-new-relationship-after-being-betrayed/

Thomas, N. (2023, March 29). *Narcissistic rage: Triggers, causes, & how to respond.* Choosing Therapy. https://www.choosingtherapy.com/narcissistic-rage/

UpJourney. (2022, July 1). *30+ reasons why narcissists come back to old relationships.* https://upjourney.com/why-do-narcissists-come-back-to-old-relationships

Venkat SR. (2022, November 9). *What is an empath?* WebMD. https://www.webmd.com/balance/what-is-an-empath

Wholesome Pathway. (2021, July 19). *How self-blame can harm you.* https://wholesomepathway.com/how-self-blame-is-harmful/

Made in the USA
Coppell, TX
14 October 2023

22830946R00068